UFOs
CAUGHT ON CAMERA! 2
SPACE BEINGS WHO APPEARED BEFORE THE MODERN SAVIOR

RYUHO OKAWA

HS PRESS

Copyright © 2021 by Ryuho Okawa
English translation © Happy Science 2021
Original title: *UFO Reading Shashinshu 2*
HS Press is an imprint of IRH Press Co., Ltd.
Tokyo
ISBN 13: 978-1-943928-15-6
ISBN 10: 1-943928-15-0

PHOTO: (p. 10-11 shooarts/p. 16-17 metamorworks/
p. 24-25 Noppasin Wongchum/p. 30-31 TitleWatsa/p. 34-35 Sergio Delle Vedove/
p. 38-39 IM_photo/p. 40-41 Imasillypirate/p. 84-85 Jakapan Kammanern/
p. 88-89 backpacking/p. 96-97 elwynn) shutterstock.com

Preface

This is an introduction of photos and video recordings of UFOs and a brief report of spiritual investigations on them.

Three or four years ago, when I heard about the president of IRH Press chasing after UFOs and trying to capture them on camera, I reprimanded him for wasting time and not focusing on increasing sale of our publications.

Later, I myself began to encounter many UFOs and to converse with the space people on board. Now, this book is the second collection of its kind.

It is not easy to differentiate the luminous objects at night whether they are UFOs, stars, or aircraft. In my case, I can detect life forms on board. Once I confirm there are vital signs inside the luminous object, I attempt to establish communications with them using remote viewing and telepathy. I investigate their origins, how many are on board, their appearances, and their purpose of visiting Earth.

In many cases, you cannot visually observe UFOs in the daylight. However, I can use my spiritual sense to find a direction in which to point the camera and more often than not the camera would capture an image of UFOs.

On the day of my great lectures, a fleet of UFOs appear in the sky above the venue. Usually, it is a large formation of between 100 to 150 UFOs. They come as security guards and also to monitor my lectures. A few of them arrive one day before the event for security purposes.

In this collection, we included images of UFOs captured around the time of my lectures in Germany and in Taiwan.

I will leave it up to the readers to decide whether these images are genuine UFOs or not, but I believe I am the only Earthling (?) who can use remote viewing to observe the inside of these UFOs and have direct conversations with space people.

Our new movie, *The Laws of the Universe–The Age of Elohim* is scheduled to be released this fall. I anticipate even more UFOs to make their appearances. Please stay tuned.

Ryuho Okawa
Master & CEO of Happy Science Group
February 13, 2021

Contents

Contents

Preface 3 • Constellation Map 10 • Layout Details 13

Part 1

Missionary Tour to Germany September – October 2018   15

UFOs in the Sky—   16

2018.9.28 Fri.

 Planet Nibiru: Marvel   18
 Planet Nix in the Small Magellanic Cloud: Liu Bei 1   19
 Planet Spicy in Canis Major   20
 Vega   21

2018.10.1 Mon.

 Titan, One of the Satellites of Saturn: Aman   22

2018.10.2 Tue.

 Planet Denken: Friedrich   23
 Planet Nix in the Small Magellanic Cloud: Liu Bei 2   24

2018 Early October | Berlin & Frankfurt

Missionary Tour to Germany   25
Master Okawa Successfully Photographed UFOs in Germany   26
 Planet Nix in the Small Magellanic Cloud: Liu Bei 3   28

2018.10.5 Fri. | Berlin

 Planet Elder in the Magellanic Galaxy: Yaidron 1 • UFOs Guiding Europe   30
Yaidron—Guardian of Justice, Protector of El Cantare   31

2018.10.9 Tue. | Frankfurt

 Planet Nix in the Small Magellanic Cloud: Liu Bei 4   32
 Planet Nibiru: Sandra   32
 Planet Sympathy in Draco Albus: Karl Jaspers   34
 Planet Engel in Pisces   36

Part 2
Space People on Mission to Protect Savior October – December 2018   37
Not All Space People Are Coming to Invade Earth   38

2018.10.21 Sun.
Planet Andalucia Beta in Ursa Minor: Mr. R (R. A. Goal)   40
R. A. Goal—Shakyamuni Buddha's Space Soul, Defender of El Cantare   41
Planet Elder in the Magellanic Galaxy: Yaidron 2   42
Planet Indole in Delphinus: Knightmayor   43

2018.10.24 Wed.
Planet Next in Cassiopeia: Millennium II   44
Mars: Hunter Queen   45

2018.10.31 Wed.
Planet Elder in the Magellanic Galaxy: Yaidron 3   46

2018.11.11 Sun.
Planet Energy in the Andromeda Galaxy: Indra   47
Planet Elder in the Magellanic Galaxy: Yaidron 4   48

2018.11.15 Thu.
Planet Elder in the Magellanic Galaxy: Yaidron 5   49
Planet Migel in Delphinus: McCartney 1   50

2018.11.20 Tue.
Planet Workthrough   51
Planet Migel in Delphinus: McCartney 2   52
Planet Engel in Pisces: Goeppels 1   53
Jupiter / Planet Mint / Planet Serpent   54

2018.11.27 Tue.
Planet Orihime in Lyra: Eternal Beauty / Moon   55

2018.12.3 Mon.
Planet Beta in the Magellanic Galaxy: Bazooka 1 /
Planet Elder in the Magellanic Galaxy: Yaidron 6 UFO Fleet   56

2018.12.8 Sat.
Planet Elder in the Magellanic Galaxy: Yaidron 7 UFO Fleet   60

2018.12.13 Thu.
Planet Elder in the Magellanic Galaxy: Yaidron 8 UFO Fleet   64

2018.12.15 Sat.
Planet Beta in the Magellanic Galaxy: Bazooka 2   70
Planet Elder in the Magellanic Galaxy: Yaidron 9 UFO Fleet   71
Planet Honeykaney in Scorpius: Mycenae   72

2018.12.19 Wed
Andromeda Galaxy   74
Planet Southern: White   75
Planet Migel in Delphinus: McCartney 3   76
Planet Santhor   77
UFO Fleet   78

2018.12.27 Thu.
From the Mother Ship near Venus   78
Planet Mohican in Capricornus: New Yorker   79

2018.12.28 Fri.
Planet Elder in the Magellanic Galaxy: Yaidron 10   80
Planet Needle in Cancer / Andromeda Galaxy   82

Part 3
The Battle between Light and Darkness January – May 2019   83
Into the Age of Cosmic-Scale Truth   84

2019.1.1 Tue.
Planet Include in Sagittarius: Metatron, Yamoozay (Yamrozay) 1   86
Metatron - the space soul of Jesus Christ who supports El Cantare   89

2019.1.2 Wed.
Planet Nix in the Small Magellanic Cloud: Liu Bei 5   90
Planet Inuyasha in Cassiopeia   91
The Fourth Planet of Pleiades (Planet Sachertorte)   92

2019.1.14 Mon.
Planet Southern: Mille-feuille   92
Planet Miguel in Delphinus: McCartney 4   93

2019.1.17 Thu.
Planet Michaeta in Pisces: Iktron / Planet Engel in Pisces: Goeppels 2   94

2019.1.23 Wed.
Planet Elder in Magellanic Galaxy: Yaidron 11   95

2019 Late February | Taipei
Master's Missionary Tour in Taiwan   96
Space people who supported Master in his missionary tour in Taiwan   97
Dragon-Shaped Clouds   98

2019.3.7 Thu.
Planet Bergius: Santos   99

2019.3.8 Fri.
Planet Elder in Magellanic Galaxy: Yaidron 12   100

2019.3.21 Thu.
Planet Include in Sagittarius: Metatron, Yamrozay 2   102
Planet Include in Sagittarius: Saitron, Semrozay   103

2019.3.24 Sun.
The Third Star (γ) in Bergius: Nichaetatron   104
The Seventh planet 'Mew' in Lyra / The Fourth Planet in the Pleiades / Planet Kirolyn in Leo / The Third Star of Bergius   105
Planet Pixel in Andromeda Galaxy: Tortootsie (Angulimala)   106

2019.4.27 Sat.
Orion: Amemiko   107
The Pleiades: Maitreya   108

2019.5.2 Thu.
(The Space Soul of) Michael   110
Planet Elder in the Magellanic Galaxy: Yaidron 13   111

Index of Space People   114
Index of Stars, Constellations, and Other Celestial Bodies   115

Constellation Map

The texts in yellow and orange on the map are of constellations and

northern celestial hemisphere

The constellations and other celestial bodies associated with the UFO readings in this book (in alphabetical order).

Andromeda Galaxy .... p. 47, 74, 82, 106	Delphinus .... p. 43, 50, 52, 76, 92
Cancer .... p. 82	Large Magellanic Cloud (Magellanic Galaxy) &
Canis Major .... p. 20	Small Magellanic Cloud ... p. 19, 24, 28, 30, 32, 42,
Capricornus .... p. 79	46, 48, 49, 56, 60, 64, 70,
Cassiopeia .... p. 44, 90	71, 80, 90, 95, 100, 111
	Leo .... p. 105
	Lyra (Vega) .... p. 21, 55, 105

other celestial bodies associated with the UFO readings in this book.

southern celestial hemisphere

```
Orion ............................................. p. 107
Pisces ........................................... p. 36, 53, 94
Sagittarius ................................... p. 86, 102
Scorpius ........................................ p. 72
Taurus (Pleiades Star Cluster) ... p. 92, 105, 108
Ursa Minor ................................... p. 40
```

[Editor's note] Regarding the UFO readings

Since the summer of 2018, Master Ryuho Okawa has been conducting UFO readings on the many UFOs that visited him. As of September 15, 2021, he has recorded 64 readings. (Additionally, many photos of UFOs were also taken.)

This book contains the UFO readings conducted between September 28, 2018 and May 2, 2019. This collection is meant to spread the fact that various space people have been sending messages to us.

In all of these cases, Master Ryuho Okawa himself discovered the UFOs. As for the video recordings, he conducted the readings on the spot. As for the photos taken, the readings were conducted at a later date.

UFO reading is an advanced spiritual ability to observe the UFOs in the sky, read space people's minds, and communicate with them using telepathy.

It is said from ancient times that those who have attained enlightenment like Shakyamuni Buddha can use abilities beyond human knowledge freely at their will, namely the Six Divine Supernatural Powers (astral travel, clairvoyance, clairaudience, mind-reading, fate-reading, and spiritual wisdom). Master Ryuho Okawa is able to use these Six Divine Supernatural Powers freely and conduct various readings.

In the reading sessions compiled in this book, Master Okawa uses the following abilities:

- **Time-travel reading**: Seeing through the subject's past and future.
- **Remote-viewing**: Sending part of the spirit body to a specific location and seeing the situation there.
- **Mind-reading**: Reading the subject's thoughts and will, including those at a remote distance.
- **Mutual conversation**: Communicating with the thoughts of various beings that are beyond human contact.

Layout Details

Pattern A: UFO readings conducted during the video recording

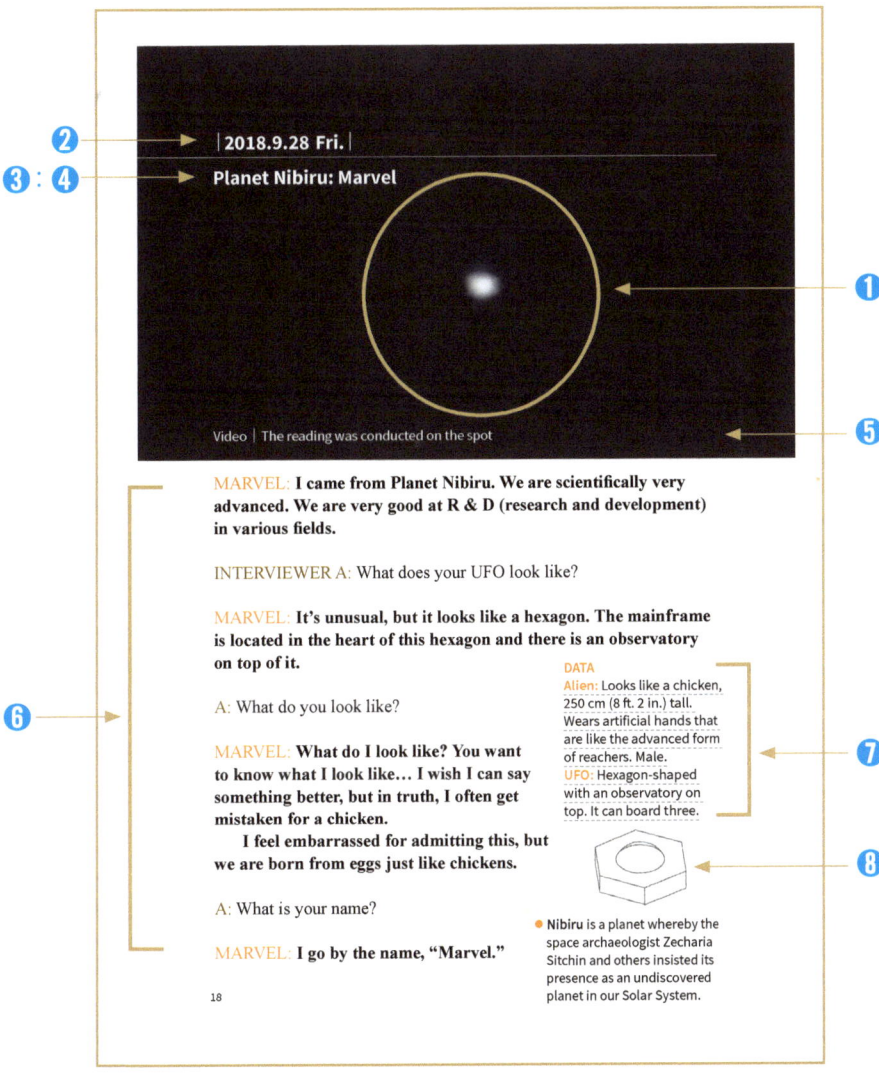

- ❶ Image of the UFO
- ❷ The date the UFO was spotted
- ❸ Where the UFO came from
- ❹ Leader's name
- ❺ The type of recording (video or photo)
- ❻ Excerpt from the reading and spiritual messages
- ❼ Characteristics of the UFO and the space people on board revealed in the reading
- ❽ Illustration of the UFO for better visual understanding

Layout Details

Pattern B: UFO readings conducted at a later date

Note: These are readings on the images cropped from the video recording or on the photos taken.

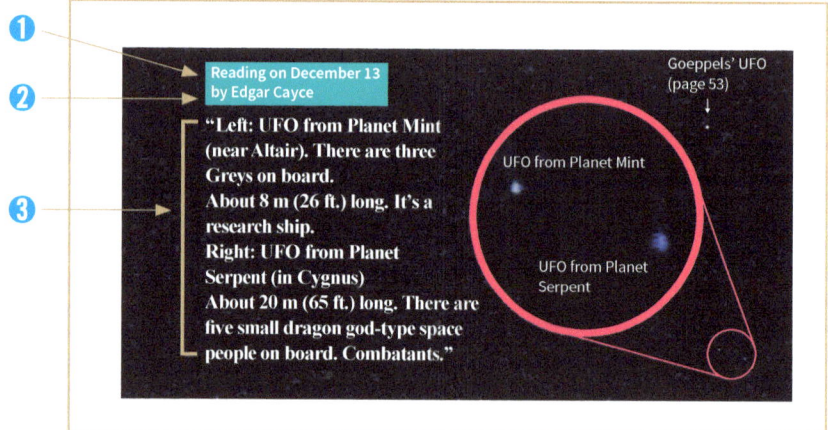

❶ Date of the reading
❷ Assisting spirits or space people who offered support in the reading
❸ Contents of the reading

■ Interviewers are symbolized as A and B.
■ Photos without location were taken around the Special Lecture Hall.
■ Only excerpts of the video recordings are included in this book.
■ Images of UFOs in this book are modified for clarity and contrast.

Part 1

September – October 2018

Missionary Tour to Germany

UFOs in the Sky

RYUHO OKAWA: Since I do not put in any special efforts to witness UFOs, I feel very sorry toward people who research UFOs. For me, I usually go out to the balcony after dinner to look up in the sky and we can spot luminous objects moving in the sky. I do not need to wait for them to appear at all. At first, I wondered if those were twinkling stars, but they were UFOs and they were moving as if they were trying to get our attention. (...)

    I do not consider UFO research to be my main occupation, so I apologize if I sound arrogant by saying how easy it is to find UFOs. But that is the reality for me. When I look up in the sky, there they are.

INTERVIEWER A: Even when there were many stars visible to our naked eyes, those stars did not appear in the video and only the light of UFOs were recorded.

RYUHO OKAWA: That's right. No stars were recorded. I think that is because UFOs are closer. (...)

I think "spiritual sense" or psychic ability is necessary to see UFOs. I use my spiritual sense to determine which direction to point the camera and take photos. Most of the time, UFOs are captured in those photos. So, I suspect it has something to do with one's level of enlightenment.

It must be my spiritual sense to let me take photos of UFOs in the daylight.

Besides, they seem to be using telepathy to contact me. Now I know I can start a dialogue with them within a second.

We also discovered that UFOs cannot remain in one spot for very long unless it is at night. During the day, they are usually moving quite wildly in the sky to avoid being detected.

In addition, we learned that UFOs are equipped with invisible mode.

I am scheduled to visit Germany in the near future. I hope to record UFOs in the German sky as well.

From *UFO Readings II*

| 2018.9.28 Fri. |

Planet Nibiru: Marvel

Video | The reading was conducted on the spot

MARVEL: **I came from Planet Nibiru. We are scientifically very advanced. We are very good at R & D (research and development) in various fields.**

INTERVIEWER A: What does your UFO look like?

MARVEL: **It's unusual, but it looks like a hexagon. The mainframe looks like a hexagon and there is an observatory on top of it.**

A: What do you look like?

MARVEL: **What do I look like? You want to know what I look like… I wish I can say something better, but in truth, I often get mistaken for a chicken.**

   I feel embarrassed for admitting this, but we are born from eggs just like chickens.

A: What is your name?

MARVEL: **I go by the name, "Marvel."**

DATA
Alien: Looks like a chicken, 250 cm (8 ft. 2 in.) tall. Wears artificial hands that are like the advanced form of reachers. Male.
UFO: Hexagon-shaped with an observatory on top. It can board three.

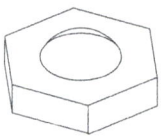

● **Nibiru** is a planet whereby the space archaeologist Zecharia Sitchin and others insisted its presence as an undiscovered planet in our Solar System.

| 2018.9.28 Fri. |

Planet Nix in the Small Magellanic Cloud: Liu Bei 1

Video | The reading was conducted on the spot

LIU BEI: **To tell you the truth, our UFO actually has a span of 2.5 km (1.5 mi). It's not the typical flying saucer, but closer to a blue whale. Most of it is invisible, but the underside has an overhang where the light is emitting.**

INTERVIEWER A: Are you the leader of this UFO?

LIU BEI: **I admire "Liu Bei Xuande" of the Eastern Han dynasty, so I go by the nickname, "Liu Bei." Our Planet Nix is very fond of the history of "The Three Kingdoms," so we come to Earth during the time of world conflicts, revolutions, wars, and founding of new countries to offer our assistance.**

 We are currently observing the present state of EU to determine what we should do about them. Since Master Ryuho Okawa will be going to Germany soon, we are looking forward to accompanying him on his trip.

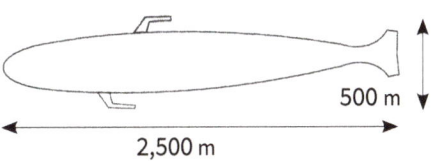

2,500 m
500 m

- **Small Magellanic Cloud** and Large Magellanic Cloud are galaxies visible in the Southern Hemisphere.

DATA
Alien: About 190 cm (6 ft. 2 in.) tall. Takes the appearance of the warlord Liu Bei Xuande.
UFO: Shape of a blue whale, 500 m (0.3 mi) wide and 2,500 m (1.5 mi) long. 30 m (98 ft.) of light-emitting section below. Supply ship-type mother ship that can store mid to small-sized aircraft.

| 2018.9.28 Fri. |

Planet Spicy in Canis Major

Video | The reading was conducted on the spot

ALIEN FROM PLANET SPICY: You must have heard of Vishnu•, one of the Hindu gods guiding India. Vishnu originally came from Canis Major. This original model of Vishnu arrived about 6,000 years ago and taught the philosophy that led to the modern Yoga, based on deep Indian philosophy.

INTERVIEWER A: What does your UFO look like?

ALIEN FROM PLANET SPICY: I suppose it looks like a magic carpet.

A: Do you eat curry?

ALIEN FROM PLANET SPICY: Yes, we do. We are vegetarian, but we are very particular about spices.

A: India is also very important.

ALIEN FROM PLANET SPICY: We must be careful not to let China take over India, Sri Lanka, and Nepal. We must protect those countries because China has their eyes on Nepal and Sri Lanka, too.

DATA
Alien: A humanoid monk. About the same height as average human. Male.
UFO: Shaped like a magic carpet. Length 25m (82ft.) x width 15m (49ft.). Five males on board.

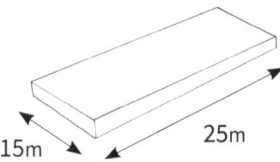
15m   25m

• Vishnu: One of the Hindu gods. According to the *Rigveda*, one of the sacred canonical texts of Brahmanism, Vishnu is the Sun god.

| 2018.9.28 Fri. |

Vega

RYUHO OKAWA: There is a blinking light. As usual, it looks like it is moving. Where did you come from? If you can respond, please tell me where you are from.

I am getting an interesting response. It says, **"I really like the book, *My Lover, Cross the Valley of Tears.*"** I wonder what it means.

INTERVIEWER A: What does it mean?

VEGAN: Master is going to Germany to do a lecture in English, right?

A: Yes.

VEGAN: We came from Vega in our support vessel. We came to support the International Headquarters.

A: I see.

VEGAN: We are an International Headquarters support vessel. The UFO that appeared earlier is another one, in some meaning.

A: Now, I understand.

VEGAN: We are cheering for other continents, too.

- **Vega** is a first-magnitude star in Lyra. UFO readings by Happy Science have revealed that Vegan people are living in multiple planets in the Vegan system, each with a highly advanced civilization.

Video | The reading was conducted on the spot

DATA
Alien: Female
UFO: Happy Science International Headquarters supporting vessel. Seven females on board.

| 2018.10.1 Mon. |

Titan, One of the Satellites of Saturn: Aman

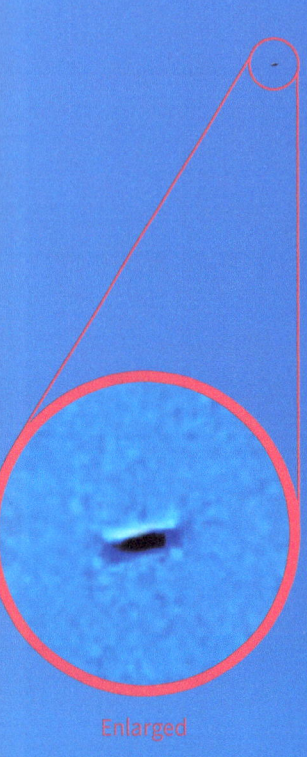

Enlarged

Reading on October 2

UFO from one of Saturn's natural satellites. It is not cylindrical, but rather shaped like a coffin with propellers on both sides as thrusters. It is used to collect samples of human beings, animals, and plants from both the land and the sea, then transport them back to the mother ship. Also, the UFO is a vessel to bring soldiers from the mother ship to Earth. It is 20 m (65 ft.) long and 5 m (16 ft.) wide. Saturnians (Titanians) are humanoids with two red protruding eyes and two antennas. They have green skin with jagged pattern. They stand upright and are about 1.8 m (5 ft. 11 in.) tall. At this time, three of them were on board. They came to research the damage caused by typhoons. They were investigating the Kanto area to see if there were any fallen rocks or trees after the storm, and intended to remove them without getting noticed. Their leader is a male named "Aman."

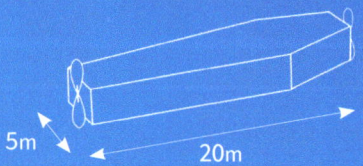

Photo

| 2018.10.2 Tue. |

Planet Denken: Friedrich

Video | The reading was conducted on the spot

RYUHO OKAWA: It is saying, **"There is a planet with a connection to Germany."** I can only hear German. Denken, Denken... It sounds like it is saying, **"Planet Denken."**

INTERVIEWER A: Planet Denken?

RYUHO OKAWA: Denken means "to think" (in German). Again, it is saying "Planet Denken." Is this a planet that thinks?

FRIEDRICH: **We have highly advanced intelligence, but our physical bodies have degraded to the point where we function mostly with our brains. Basically, our bodies are just our heads and small appendages attached to them. So, on our planet, most of the physical tasks are done by cyborgs.**

RYUHO OKAWA: Where is Planet Denken located?

[*About five seconds of silence.*]

FRIEDRICH: **Actually, this location is still unknown to you. In fact, the Milky Way is not the center of the universe. It is actually a bit off center, but our planet is closer to the center of the universe.**

A: Is it the planet where Immanuel Kant• came from?

FRIEDRICH: **Yes, it is.**

A: So, are you currently observing Chancellor Merkel?

FRIEDRICH: **Yes, we are. In fact, that is how we are able to establish this link to be here to say our greetings.**

A: Thank you for coming from Germany.

FRIEDRICH: **We will see you in Germany. We are looking forward to it.**

● **Immanuel Kant** (1724 ~ 1804)
German philosopher. Spiritual research by Happy Science has revealed that he has been reborn as Angela Merkel, the first female chancellor of Germany. Refer to *Spiritual Interview with the Guardian Spirit of Angela Merkel* [Tokyo: HS Press, 2018].

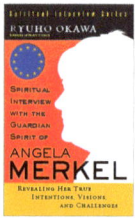

DATA
Alien: It is virtually just a head with small limbs attached to it. It looks like an octopus about 1.5 heads tall.

| 2018.10.2 Tue. |

Planet Nix in the Small Magellanic Cloud: Liu Bei 2

The day before Master's departure for Germany, a UFO from Planet Nix appeared again.

2018 Early October | Berlin & Frankfurt

 Missionary Tour to Germany

Master Okawa visited Germany at the beginning of October. On Oct. 7, he gave a lecture in English titled, "Love for the Future" and held a Q & A session. Master showed the way for Germany to move forward after facing many problems stemming from the defeat in the 20th century wars. Several photos and videos of UFOs were recorded before and after Master's lecture.

● Since 2007, Master Ryuho Okawa has energetically gone on missionary tours in Japan and the world. He has already visited the five continents.

The English lecture given on Oct. 7, 2018, in Master's missionary tour to Germany

"Love for the Future"

At The Ritz-Carlton, Berlin

> Stop the world war
> And let the people believe in God.
> And live as God loves them.

- From Chapter One, "Love for the Future" in *Love for the Future* [New York: IRH Press, 2019]

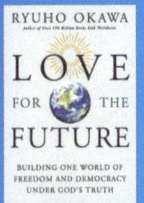

Master Okawa Successfully Photographed UFOs in Germany

UFOs began to appear quite frequently in Japan. Then, another one appeared on the night before we left for Germany, so I took a video and picture and spoke to the alien on board. He said, "See you tomorrow in Germany." I wondered if it could happen or not.

    The hotel we stayed in Germany was faced in such a way that when I opened the window of my room, I could only see the Brandenburg Gate side. Despite the limited view at night, I found the same UFO we saw in Minato Ward of Tokyo, Japan, hovering just above the Brandenburg Gate. I was very surprised to see it being stationary in the sky. The alien said they would come and escort me to Germany and they really did. (...)

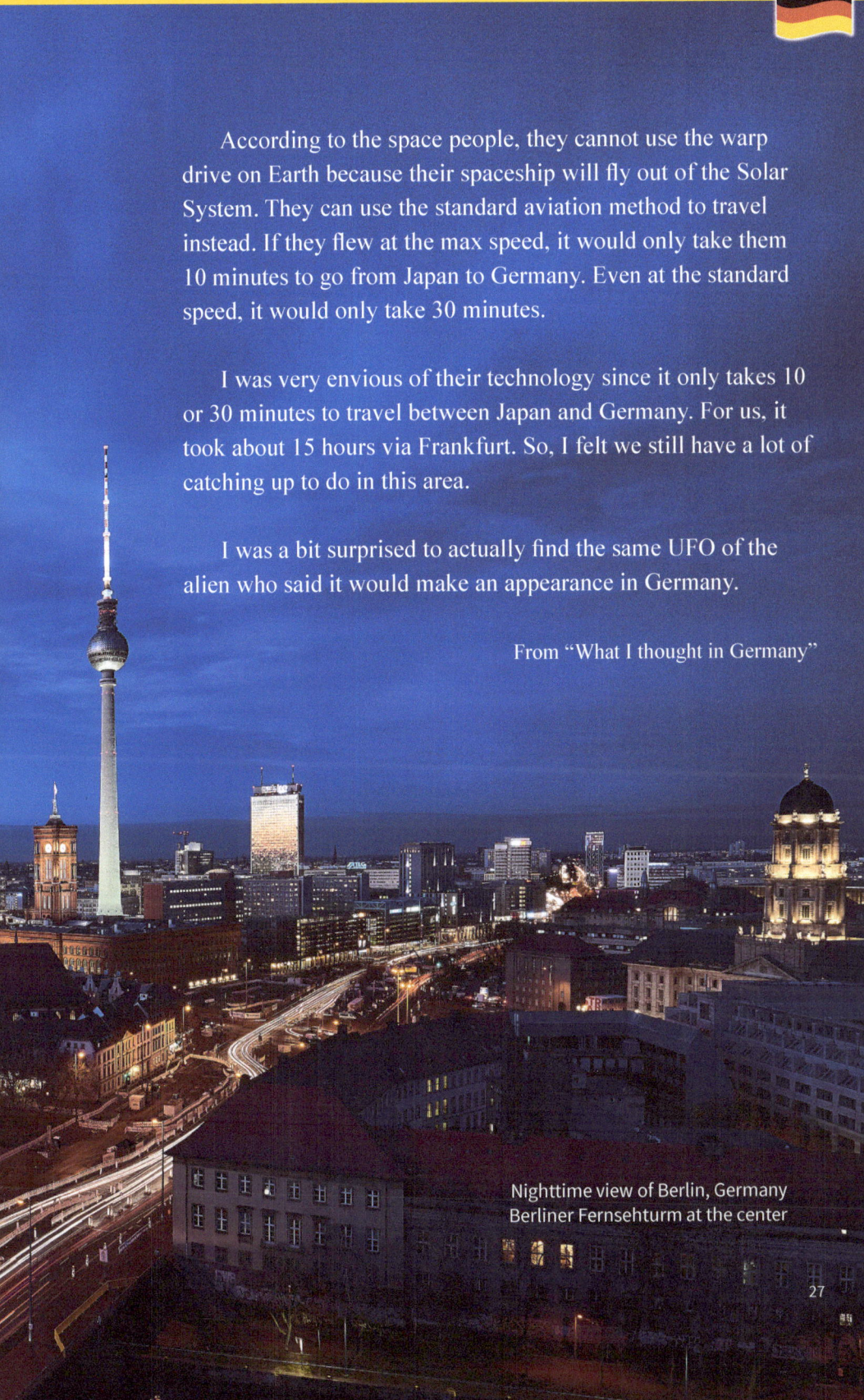

According to the space people, they cannot use the warp drive on Earth because their spaceship will fly out of the Solar System. They can use the standard aviation method to travel instead. If they flew at the max speed, it would only take them 10 minutes to go from Japan to Germany. Even at the standard speed, it would only take 30 minutes.

I was very envious of their technology since it only takes 10 or 30 minutes to travel between Japan and Germany. For us, it took about 15 hours via Frankfurt. So, I felt we still have a lot of catching up to do in this area.

I was a bit surprised to actually find the same UFO of the alien who said it would make an appearance in Germany.

From "What I thought in Germany"

Nighttime view of Berlin, Germany
Berliner Fernsehturm at the center

2018.10.3 Wed. | Berlin

Planet Nix in the Small Magellanic Cloud: Liu Bei 3

RYUHO OKAWA: Are you a UFO or not?

[*About five seconds of silence.*]

LIU BEI: **As promised, we are here to welcome you.**

INTERVIEWER A: Are you Liu Bei from Planet Nix? (Refer to page 19.)

LIU BEI: **Yes, we are here to pay our respects. We are hovering at about 100 m (328 ft.) to 150 m (492 ft.) in the air, so this is quite risky for us. There are many helicopters and balloons at this height.**

RYUHO OKAWA: It is the same type of light as the one we saw in Tokyo. Is it orange? You said you will come see us again and you really did.

A: It looks like it is changing colors.

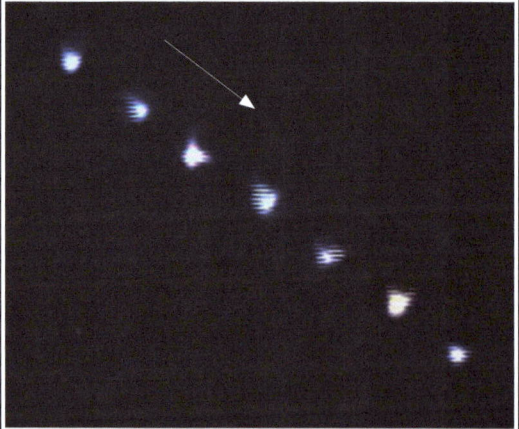

Position and color at 37 seconds and every 10 seconds thereafter.

Video | The reading was conducted on the spot

RYUHO OKAWA: It looks orange to the naked eye.

LIU BEI: Yes, we are here to escort you.

A: OK. We are looking forward to your support during our stay.

LIU BEI: We are just above the Brandenburg Gate.

RYUHO OKAWA: This is authentic. It is the same as the one we saw yesterday in Tokyo.

A: It is the real one. Thank you very much.

Enlarged image

| 2018.10.5 Fri. | Berlin |

Planet Elder in the Magellanic Galaxy: Yaidron 1/ UFOs Guiding Europe

Position and color at 22 seconds and every 2 seconds thereafter.

Video | The reading was conducted on the spot

RYUHO OKAWA: We are currently recording your UFO. Could you please let me know who you are? [*About 10 seconds of silence.*]

He says, **"I am your Yaidron."**

INTERVIEWER A: Oh! Mr. Yaidron. Thank you very much for guarding us.

YAIDRON: We were concerned about your safety, so we are here to check on you.

A: I want to thank you from the bottom of my heart.

YAIDRON: We are here to protect the Lord, so that he can fulfill his mission. We will also protect your mind.

A: Thank you again for coming to protect us, it is very reassuring.

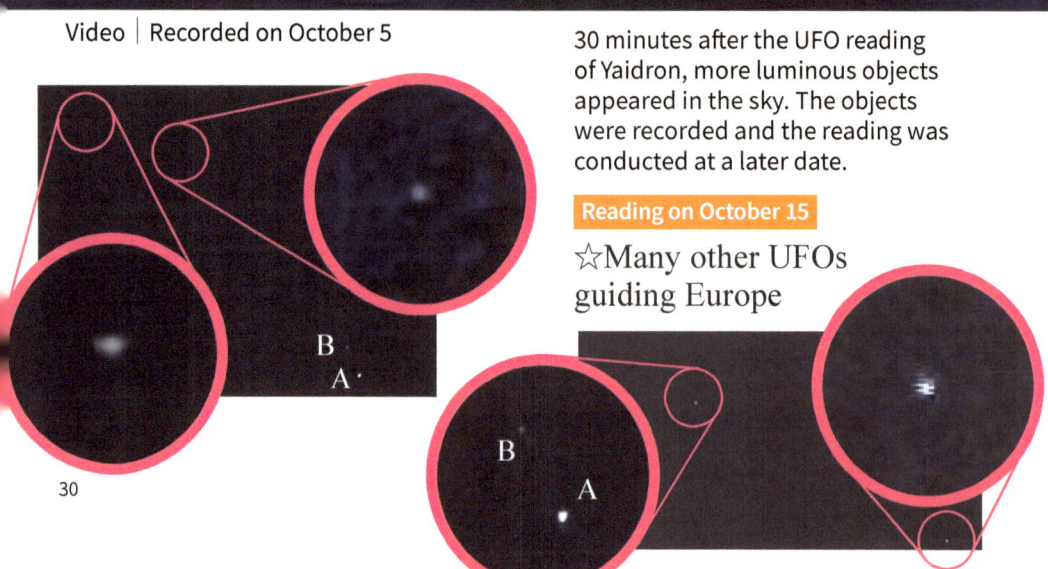

Video | Recorded on October 5

30 minutes after the UFO reading of Yaidron, more luminous objects appeared in the sky. The objects were recorded and the reading was conducted at a later date.

Reading on October 15

☆Many other UFOs guiding Europe

Yaidron—Guardian of Justice, Protector of El Cantare

Yaidron's UFO was first photographed on August 4, 2018. Since then, Yaidron has appeared in many UFO readings and spiritual messages. He is a space being from Planet Elder in the Magellanic Galaxy. He is an immortal existence who transcends both physical and spiritual bodies. He has been overseeing the rise and fall of civilizations, wars, and major disasters on Earth. Yaidron possesses powers that are similar to those of high spirits in the Earth's Spirit World and is a god of justice-like being. On Elder, he works as someone like the chief justice and highest-ranking statesman and is in charge of justice and judgment. In the past, Yaidron was taught by El Cantare on a Messiah-training planet and is currently protecting Master Ryuho Okawa, who is the human incarnation of El Cantare.

Large Magellanic Cloud (Left), Small Magellanic Cloud (Right)

Since August 2018, Yaidron has been sending numerous messages. (Few are mentioned below.)

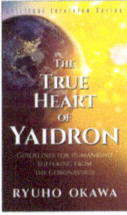 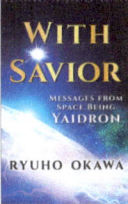

Spiritual messages from Yaidron are recorded in **The True Heart of Yaidron** [Tokyo: HS Press, 2021](left) and **With Savior: Messages from Space Being Yaidron** [Tokyo: HS Press, 2020] (right).

With Savior — We are now living together with Savior

Savior and Master of the Universe, Lord El Cantare. This is a new Gospel to spread the fact that we are now living together with Savior. The names "Yaidron" and his wife "Namiel" appear in the lyrics. This is a majestic song to encourage humankind on the cosmic scale.

DVD CD "With Savior"
Words & Music by Ryuho Okawa, Arrangement by Sayaka Okawa and Yuichi Mizusawa, Song by Sayaka Okawa (See p. 129)

| 2018.10.9 Tue. | Frankfurt |

Planet Nix in the Small Magellanic Cloud: Liu Bei 4

RYUHO OKAWA: In the afternoon of October 9, 2018, I took a picture at the observatory of the Main Tower in Frankfurt, Germany. I pointed the camera toward where I sensed something spiritual and took a picture. In the picture, there is an image of an unusual shape resembling a magic carpet or a spring roll, so I will conduct a spiritual reading to find out what it is.

[*About five seconds of silence.*]

LIU BEI: **We are from "Planet Liu Bei Xuande" (Planet Nix). Previously, you saw us in Tokyo. This time, we are in a midsized vessel. It is about 30 m (98 ft.) long and consists of two parts linked together.**

We were there to say our final farewell and to offer security and protection. I thought you would like to find us again, so we tried to fly close by. I am very happy you could capture our presence.

DATA
UFO: Midsized vessel, 25 ~ 30 m (82 ~ 98 ft.) long and 5 ~ 6 m (16 ~ 20 ft.) high. Two square parts linked together, each with two floors. There are 15 on board.

| 2018.10.9 Tue. | Frankfurt |

Planet Nibiru: Sandra

Reading on November 22

☆Planet Nibiru: Leader is a female named Sandra. There are three on board. It is 13 m (43 ft.) in diameter and 3 m (10 ft.) high. Humanoid aliens. Their vessel was in the invisible mode, but it showed up in the photo. They were also recording Master's activities.

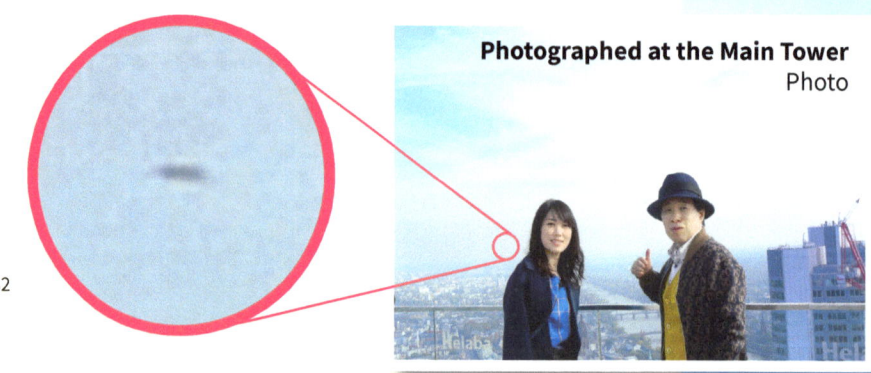

Photographed at the Main Tower
Photo

INTERVIEWER A: Where is the mother ship?

LIU BEI: The mother ship is flying at a very high altitude because otherwise, it would be too easy to be detected during the day, but we are at a few hundred meters (about 1,000 ft.).

We thought your missionary tour in Germany was a great success. We recorded your lecture and broadcasted it. Congratulations.

I am optimistic that your movement will expand. We will help from above by sending down inspirations to move more and more people. We will put more effort to gather people who have connections to this movement.

Photo | The reading was conducted later on the same day

Enlarged image

The picture was taken at the Main Tower in Frankfurt Germany.

The Main Tower is located at the center of the city. It is the fourth highest skyscraper in the city at 198 m (650 ft.). Its rooftop observatory offers a panoramic view of the city.

| 2018.10.9 Tue. | Frankfurt |

Planet Sympathy in Draco Albus: Karl Jaspers

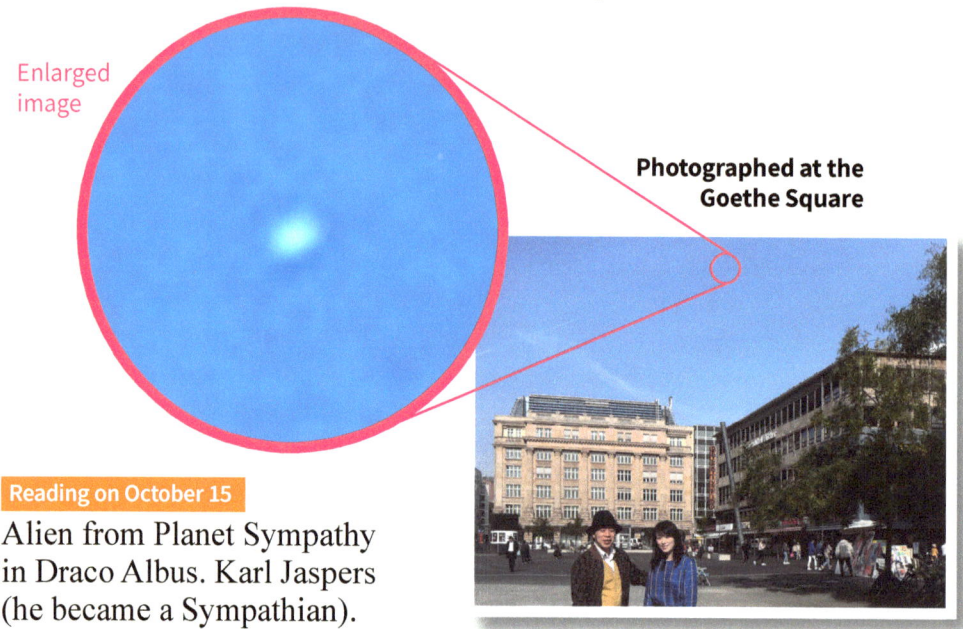

Enlarged image

Photographed at the Goethe Square

Reading on October 15

Alien from Planet Sympathy in Draco Albus. Karl Jaspers (he became a Sympathian).

Reading on the picture taken at the Goethe Square.

RYUHO OKAWA: Oh, Rient Arl Croud*, please assist us with our **UFO reading**.

INTERVIEWER A: On October 9, 2018, we took a picture at the Goethe Square in Frankfurt, Germany. When we enlarged the picture, we saw something that looked like a UFO. Could you tell us something about this object?

RIENT ARL CROUD: Hmm... I see the name, **"Jaspers."** He says, **"I graduated from Earth."**

A: Oh? Are you an alien with some connections to Mr. Jaspers' soul? Or are you Mr. Jaspers himself?

- **Rient Arl Croud**: One of the soul siblings of El Cantare, God of the Earth. Croud was a king of ancient Inca about 7,000 years ago. In the heavenly world, he has full authority over all matters involving space people and Earth.

DATA
Alien: They perceive themselves as humanoids.
UFO: It looks like a brain.

Karl Jaspers (1883 ~ 1969)
German philosopher and psychiatrist. One of the representatives of existentialism.

The Goethe Square
The square is located along the financial district of Frankfurt. There is a bronze statue of Johann Wolfgang Goethe, a Frankfurt-born German poet.

JASPERS: **There is a planet called Sympathy in Draco Albus, and I have become one of its people.**

A: You mentioned that you have "graduated," but what does that mean? Is there a certification?

JASPERS: **Every year, there are about 10 to 20 people who complete their reincarnations on Earth. Those people have learned what they could as Earthlings and are ready to move on.**

I have graduated from Earth as a philosopher, but I still have one regret which is to witness whether the Laws of El Cantare can change the Earth or not. So, even now I like to come back to gather additional information.

INTERVIEWER B: Is there God on Planet Sympathy?

JASPERS: **My understanding is that God is connected to other planets in the universe by "sympathy." I would say something like a computer database linked to other databases in a sense, but not quite the same. In some ways, our God is like the "Symphony of the Universe" playing the tunes of the universe.**

This missionary tour is carefully observed by many who have connections to Germany. Please be aware that this mission is a critical one. There may have been only a limited number of audiences at the lecture this time, however, the fact that Master Ryuho Okawa came to the 21st century Germany and offered his overall evaluation of post-war Germany has a great significance. It is highly likely that the world trend will change from now on based on the information Master gave.

| 2018.10.9 Tue. | Frankfurt |

Planet Engel in Pisces

Video | The reading was conducted on the spot

RYUHO OKAWA: I'm hearing, **"Engelians."** If you have any questions, go ahead.

INTERVIEWER A: Which constellation are you from?

ENGELIAN: **Pisces.**

A: What do you look like?

ENGELIAN: **Umm... our hands are shaped like scissors, but our legs are like human's. We have goat-like horns that face up and outward.**

A: What values are important to you?

ENGELIAN: **We are eco-conscious. So, we are guiding people to be more eco-friendly now. Because of our guidance, German people are very conscious of not being wasteful and making efforts to prevent further global warming. Japanese people don't seem to have much concern, though.**

DATA
Alien: Combination of goat and crawfish, with two human-like legs, goat-like horns, and scissors-like hands.
UFO: Energy-saving flying saucer, 8 m (26 ft.) in diameter and 2 ~ 3 m (7 ~ 10 ft.) high. It can board three.

This alien was later identified as "Goeppels" by an additional UFO reading. (Refer to page 53.)

Part 2

October – December 2018

Space People on Mission to Protect Savior

Not All Space People Are Coming to Invade Earth

I believe there is a chance that some space people will partially invade Earth at least once during the 21st century. People will witness the likely scenarios of Hollywood movies in real life; however, Earth will not be conquered one-sidedly.

In that sense, I think it is possible to increase people's awareness of this by showing movies like *The Laws of the Universe -Part I*. Some space people have been visiting Earth since ancient times, and there are some who have assimilated on Earth. There are also some who have been watching over Earth for a long time. Informing people of this will help them realize that not all space people are here to conquer Earth.

So, while there is a possibility of partial invasion or something similar, I think earthlings will try to defend themselves, and there are groups of space people who want to protect Earth. Therefore, by joining our forces, we will be able to protect Earth. That is my thinking at this time.

From the lecture, "What I Thought in Germany"

RYUHO OKAWA: He says **"I am indeed Mr. R from Andalucia."**

INTERVIEWER A: You are a messiah-class being.

MR. R: **Most likely, both Japan and the U.S. will soon be flooded with reports of UFO and space people sightings.**

A: Can you elaborate on how the future society would be like?

MR. R: **What comes next is the matter of discerning information. There must be a service that helps sift through all the information instead of the giant mass media corporations. In the future society, people will depend on the business where the quality of information is distinguished instantaneously through computers.**

    In addition, people will go beyond that and step into the world of supernatural powers without a doubt.

> DATA
> UFO: Maximum diameter is 50 m (164 ft.).
> Shape of a chandelier (half of a sphere). Dangling parts on the underside are lighting up.

R. A. Goal—Shakyamuni Buddha's Space Soul, Defender of El Cantare

R. A. Goal is one of the commanders of the space defense force. He is a space being with a certified messiah status. He is from Planet Andalucia Beta in Ursa Minor. During the spiritual message session on January 30, 2021, he was revealed to be one of the space souls of Shakyamuni Buddha. Since September 16, 2018, he has made numerous appearances in UFO readings and spiritual message sessions. R. A. Goal is in charge of protecting El Cantare, who has descended to earth as Ryuho Okawa. He has the characteristics of a religious leader and also has the ability to create an advanced civilization on a planetary scale. He is also referred to as Mr. R or Master R.

Since September 2018, R. A. Goal has been sending numerous messages. (Few are mentioned below.)

Warnings against the global pandemic of novel coronavirus originating from China since January 2020

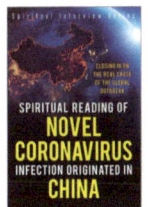 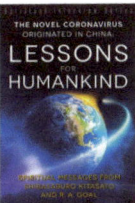

Spiritual Reading of Novel Coronavirus Infection Originated in China [Tokyo: HS Press, 2020] (left) and ***The Novel Coronavirus Originated in China: Lessons for Humankind*** [Tokyo: HS Press, 2020] (right) revealed that this coronavirus is a biological weapon manufactured by China. They also contain warnings about the global pandemic.

| 2018.10.21 Sun. |

Planet Elder in the Magellanic Galaxy: Yaidron 2

Video | The reading was conducted on the spot

INTERVIEWER A: As expected, Yaidron is always protecting us. I have been wondering how you are making a living.

YAIDRON: **We are actually based on "Anima• Economy." We accumulate anima.**

When we win interplanetary wars, we gain many anima. We have something like "anima savings." We can work as much as our anima savings allow.

A: Do you ever interact with the spiritual world or the heavenly world?

YAIDRON: **Yes, we do. However, only the qualified can interact with us.**

It means that, at the least, they must be able to travel between planets as a soul. We use the 8th dimensional wormholes to travel between planets.

A: I think you have "Love" within you.

YAIDRON: **I surely hope so, since I am also a Guardian God.**

• **Anima**: souls and spirits of living creatures.

| 2018.10.21 Sun. |

Planet Indole in Delphinus: Knightmayor

RYUHO OKAWA: This is a new one. It says it is from **Planet Indole**.

KNIGHTMAYOR: **We often appeared in Peru. It is relatively rare for us to be in this part of the world. We have a close relationship with King Rient Arl Croud.**

INTERVIEWER A: What kind of planet is Indole?

KNIGHTMAYOR: **We are herbivores.**

 We had brought many vegetables to Earth: yacón, pumpkin, potato, sweet potato, cucumber, tomato, and so on.

 We brought peace to Earth by bringing these vegetables. Ample food supply can cease disputes and conflicts.

 Many different types of space people had contributed to building civilizations on Earth. I wish Earthlings would show more appreciation to all the benefits they received from the great universe.

DATA
Alien: Grasshopper-like jagged teeth and two antennas. They are male and female, wearing blue or red space suit. They seem like astronauts.
UFO: Disk-type UFO, 80 m (262 ft.) in radius.

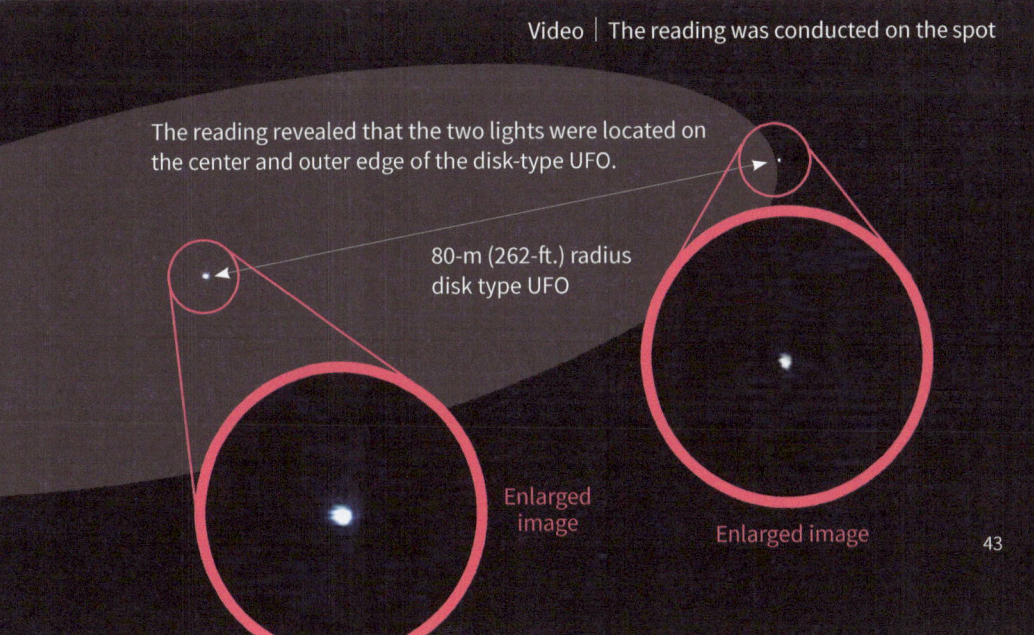

Video | The reading was conducted on the spot

The reading revealed that the two lights were located on the center and outer edge of the disk-type UFO.

80-m (262-ft.) radius disk type UFO

Enlarged image

Enlarged image

43

2018.10.24 Wed.

Planet Next in Cassiopeia: Millennium II

A UFO belonging to space people with connection to Hamerton appeared in the night sky of Oct. 24, 2018. Earlier in the day, "Spiritual Messages from Hamerton – Can the Intellectual Life Be Established in Modern Times?" was recorded at the Happy Science General Headquarters.

Position at 240 seconds and every 30 seconds thereafter

Video | The reading was conducted on the spot

INTERVIEWER A: What do you look like?

MILLENNIUM II: I have two heads.

Normally, you have two brains—the left brain and the right brain, but for us, each side of the brain developed separately and has its own head. Right brain is the creative, artistic side, and left brain is the analytical, mechanical processing side. For those of us from Planet Next, both of our brains collaborate with each other.

It is important to get those brains to work together.

They must be well balanced. They check each other when deciding what is right. What is right from the religious and practical standpoints should not be too different from each other. It is important to fuse those values and find the one unified path.

We want people to know that training is very important because training and inspiration are directly proportional to each other.

DATA
Alien: Humanoid with advanced "right brain" and "left brain" in two separate heads. One torso with two arms and two legs. Male.

| 2018.10.24 Wed. |

Mars: Hunter Queen

Video | The reading was conducted on the spot

RYUHO OKAWA: It looks like it is sending us a sign.
It says **"I am from Mars."**

HUNTER QUEEN: **Mars is often associated with war and called the Planet of War. It is thought to have influence on wars. Indeed, we did have such a period in our history.**

In fact, Mars has certain factors that tend to cause wars. In the spiritual sense, there is a spiritual magnetic field which tends to cause conflicts. So, when Mars has stronger influence on Earth, there will be more dispute and strife.

It has not been too long since the civilization on Mars perished.

There was a civilization on the continent of Lemuria which originally came from Mars.

INTERVIEWER A: What is the difference between Martians and Reptilians?

HUNTER QUEEN: **I'm a humanoid and I have the combat skills to fight against Reptilians. In essence, we are soldiers.**

DATA
Alien: A Wonder Woman-like humanoid. She can fly if the gravity is not too strong.
UFO: It can board 15.

| 2018.10.31 Wed. |

Planet Elder in the Magellanic Galaxy: Yaidron 3

INTERVIEWER A: Today's UFO is flickering a lot, isn't it?

YAIDRON: Yes, it is. I wanted to let you know we are here.
Before long, Savior's existence will be known on the global scale.
You have been sending out the message that he is not only the Savior but also the God of the Earth. This is a very powerful message.

A: Is there God on Planet Elder?

YAIDRON: There is "God of Progress." This being may possibly be a branch soul of El Cantare.
We call our God "Maitrey."
Today, I wanted to cheer you up. Don't think small and feel discouraged. The great cogwheel of the global scale will begin to turn in the next few years. Please be ready to endure the Earth-level movement.

DATA
UFO: 50 m (164 ft.) long. Midsized ship shaped like *dorayaki* (two pancakes with sweet fillings in between). About 30 on board. There is a 300-m (984-ft.) mother ship and an even larger mother ship. Yaidron changed ships from the large mother ship to the midsized ship before showing up.

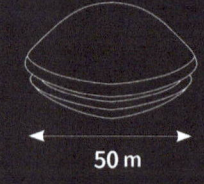

50 m

Positions at 372 seconds and every 3 seconds thereafter. It continued to move while flashing.

Video | The reading was conducted on the spot

| 2018.11.11 Sun. |

Planet Energy in the Andromeda Galaxy: Indra

Video | The reading was conducted on the spot

RYUHO OKAWA: This is a Godzilla-style alien from Planet Energy in the Andromeda Galaxy.

INDRA: **We were developed and raised as countermeasures for Reptilians. When Reptilians commit crimes, we the police will apprehend them.**

INTERVIEWER A: What is your name?

INDRA: **I'm Indra. Shakra Devanam Indra. I used to appear around Buddha. Indra is on guard. Ancient people had no knowledge of space people, so when I appeared they thought one of the Hindu gods had appeared.**

A: I believe the Great Ame-no-Mioya-Gami resides in Andromeda Galaxy.

INDRA: **Yes, I still serve him.**
　Ame-no-Mioya-Gami looks like a giant Sumo wrestler with a very distinguished face and makeup like Kabuki actors. He is about 25 m (82 ft.) tall.

DATA
Alien: About 2.5 m (8 ft. 2 in.) tall. Looks like a dark green Godzilla. A wild animal was altered artificially. Male.
UFO: Small sized ship with a diameter of 80 m (265 ft.) and height of 15 m (49 ft.). There are 65 on board.

• Andromeda Galaxy: Located approximately 2.5 million light-years from the Milky Way Galaxy.

| 2018.11.11 Sun. |

Planet Elder in the Magellanic Galaxy: Yaidron 4

INTERVIEWER A: On Earth, Moses used similar power to divide the sea. Does he have a connection to your planet?

YAIDRON: **Moses was a type of magician. His magic was more for the earthly use compared to ours.**

Our powers are at the universal level. "Magic of the universe" is much more beyond the limit.

In outer space, there are still unknown energies and matters that are part of the entire universe. Recently, you are hearing about dark matter, but there are other matter you have yet to discover. We can freely use all such matters.

A: Recently, we have learned about "Maitrey." (Refer to page 46.)

YAIDRON: **Maitrey is another form of mercy. There was Mithraism, which became the origin of Maitrey belief. It used to be worshiped in the area now known as Iran. Maitrey is a goddess. She had appeared in that part of the world.**

Video | The reading was conducted on the spot

| 2018.11.15 Thu. |

Planet Elder in the Magellanic Galaxy: Yaidron 5

Video | The reading was conducted on the spot

On Nov. 15, 2018, "Spiritual Message of Mao Zedong" was recorded. In the session, it was revealed that Mao Zedong, the founding father of the People's Republic of China, had become one of the top devils on Earth with connections to the dark universe. A UFO reading was conducted the same evening.

YAIDRON: **I had been suspecting that idolatry (idol worship) is something that needs to be destroyed. For China, as long as people worship Mao Zedong, he will be protected. So, we must make it very clear that he is not to be respected or worshiped.**

It is your mission to fight against him.

Today, you have revealed he is the number one devil in hell as of recent. There might have been a different one in the ancient times, but you made a great achievement to discover that he has become the worst of the worst and that he has connections to the dark universe.

This is a problem on the global scale.

| 2018.11.15 Thu. |

Planet Migel in Delphinus: McCartney 1

Video | The reading was conducted on the spot

INTERVIEWER A: Did you come here because you have a message for us?

MCCARTNEY: **I want to tell you that we are hoping for a revival of heroes because Earth is in need of heroes. It means those who can tell good from bad, defeat evil, and help the people.**
   People on our planet focus on martial arts training. Planet Migel is the root of all kinds of martial arts.

A: Are there any famous people from your planet?

MCCARTNEY: **Bruce Lee and Mifune of the World.**

A: Do you have other messages?

MCCARTNEY: **I want to tell you that muscle strength generates the force that repels Ikiryo (evil spirit of a living person) and evil spirits.**
   It is important to spend time studying, but that is not enough. Although it's difficult, you must train both mentally and physically to be a real hero.

DATA
Alien: 2.3 m (7 ft. 7 in.) tall, weighs 120 kg (265 lb.), humanoid male.
UFO: Diamond-shaped with a protruded second floor. It can board 30.

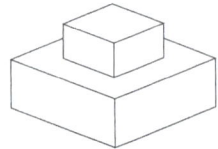

| 2018.11.20 Tue. |

Planet Workthrough

RYUHO OKAWA: Who is there? [*About 10 seconds of silence.*]
I hear "**Planet Workthrough.**" I wonder if "Workthrough" means to "skip" work.
Is this a planet of lazy people?

ALIEN FROM WORKTHROUGH: **We have been promoting "don't work too hard movement." Mainly, we focus on the advanced nations to increase more vacation time for them.**

RYUHO OKAWA: Do you have something you want to tell us?

ALIEN FROM WORKTHROUGH: **Well, let's lighten up the workload for everyone and enjoy life slowly and abundantly.**

INTERVIEWER A: What do you look like?

ALIEN FROM WORKTHROUGH: **I am always laying down on my side and propped on one elbow.**
I am a vegetarian. Carnivorous life forms are very combative and they make the world very harsh, so we are promoting the plant-based lifestyle.

DATA
Alien: Human face with sheep-like round horns. Wearing a loose, woolly loungewear.

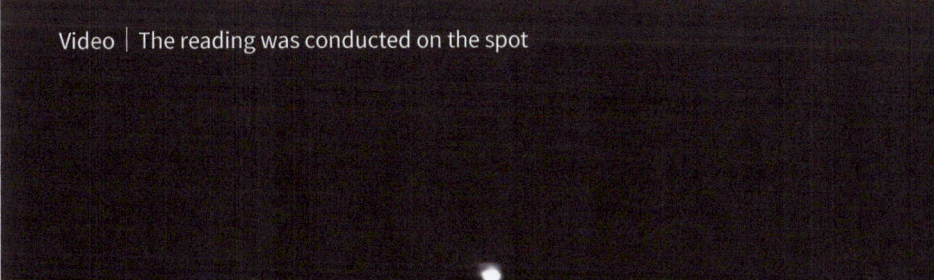
Video | The reading was conducted on the spot

| 2018.11.20 Tue. |

Planet Migel in Delphinus: McCartney 2

Video | The reading was conducted on the spot

RYUHO OKAWA: It says "**Migel.**" Is this "McCartney"?

MCCARTNEY: **Heroes are not just those who fight in battles. There are heroes in music, theater, and other forms of acting. Singers and actors can be heroes. Heroes can be found in the field of art.**

INTERVIEWER A: Do you actually have a connection to the Beatles?

MCCARTNEY: **Hahaha [*laughs*]. Maybe I do.**
   I believe John Lennon has been offering his spiritual support for your music. I suggest you do a spiritual reading on him to find out more about him. I do not wish to divulge too much, but he may have an unexpected mission. He truly wished to save the people all around the world.

At a later date, "Spiritual Messages from John Lennon" is recorded. In the session, it was revealed that John Lennon is a branch spirit of Jesus Christ.

Refer to *John Lennon's Message from Heaven* [Tokyo: HS Press, 2020].

| 2018.11.20 Tue. |

Planet Engel in Pisces: Goeppels 1

Video | The reading was conducted on the spot

RYUHO OKAWA: I think it is saying "**Planet Engel.**"

INTERVIEWER A: I think this is the same UFO that appeared in Frankfurt, Germany. (Refer to page 36.)

GOEPPELS: **I am here to tell you something in regards to the problems of Thailand. I know Thailand is trying to make progress, but their religion is at a standstill. They may think they are fighting against atheism and materialism of a communist country like China, but unfortunately, their Hinayana Buddhism teaches something like a "no Buddha theory."**

A: Yes, they do.

GOEPPELS: **I'm also concerned about saving energy. You should think about energy efficiency when it comes to your missionary activities. You should select places where the teaching of the Truth is more likely to spread widely.**

   Let's focus your energy on the 20% to produce 80% of results. Determine which countries will be the priority 20% and emphasize your effort there rather than trying to cover all of them.

DATA
UFO: Dual structure: top and bottom parts.
It resembles a hamburger. There are 3 on board.

| 2018.11.20 Tue. |

Jupiter / Planet Mint / Planet Serpent

In the video recording of the UFO from Planet Migel in Delphinus (page 52), another luminous object was observed. A UFO reading was conducted at a later date to investigate the object.

Reading on December 13 by Edgar Cayce

"Midsized ship from Jupiter. Shaped like a spinning wheel. It is 25 m (98 ft.) long and 10 m (32 ft.) wide. (It can board 30.) Humanoids."

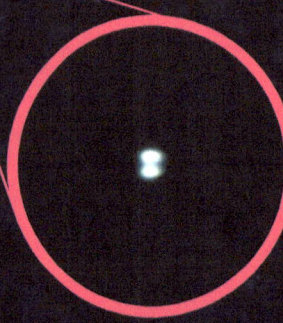
UFO from Jupiter
Video

McCartney's UFO (page 52)

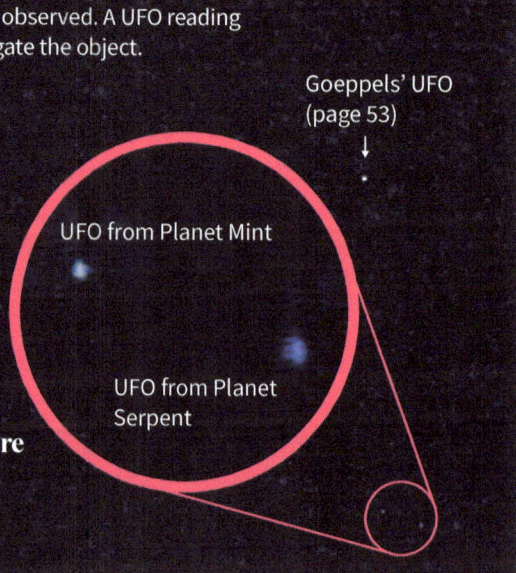
25 m
10 m

In the video recording of the UFO from Planet Engel in Pisces (page 53), another luminous object was observed. A UFO reading was conducted at a later date to investigate the object.

Video

Reading on December 13 by Edgar Cayce

Goeppels' UFO (page 53)

"Left: UFO from Planet Mint (near Altair). There are three Greys on board.
About 8 m (26 ft.) long. It's a research ship.
Right: UFO from Planet Serpent (in Cygnus).
About 20 m (65 ft.) long. There are five small dragon god-type space people on board. Combatants."

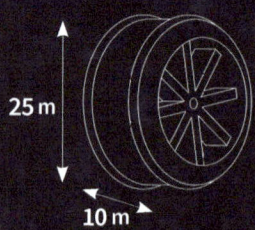
UFO from Planet Mint
UFO from Planet Serpent

● **Edgar Cayce** (1877 ~ 1945): An American prophet and spiritual healer who conducted numerous readings while being in a hypnotic state. Also known as "the Sleeping Prophet."

| 2018.11.27 Tue. |

Planet Orihime in Lyra: Eternal Beauty / Moon

RYUHO OKAWA: I hear a voice saying she is "**Nukata-no-O-Kimi.**" She says "**I also have connection to the universe.**"

ETERNAL BEAUTY: In the universe, there was the original story of Orihime (Vega) who is now known in the Japanese legend of Orihime and Hikoboshi (Altair).

    This time, El Cantare descended to earth on July 7. July 7 is when a ladder comes down from the heavenly world.

    We sometimes come down for a short time to teach the concept of "eternity" and then return to the heavenly world.

DATA
Alien: Looks like an oriental heavenly maiden with her hair in a butterfly knot. Female.
UFO: Shaped like a double helix, as if two rice bowls were put together on their bottoms. There are 50 on board.

Eternal Beauty's UFO

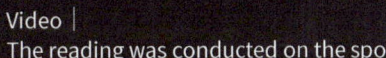

Video |
The reading was conducted on the spot

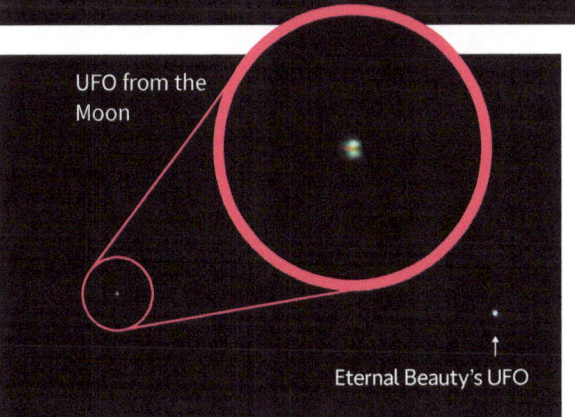

UFO from the Moon

Eternal Beauty's UFO

Video

In the video recording of Eternal Beauty's UFO, another luminous object was observed. A UFO reading was conducted at a later date to investigate the object.

Reading on December 13 by Edgar Cayce

"Research ship from the Moon. It can board 10. There are two humanoids and eight Greys."

| 2018.12.3 Mon. |

Planet Beta in the Magellanic Galaxy: Bazooka 1
Planet Elder in the Magellanic Galaxy: Yaidron 6 UFO Fleet

UFO of "Bazooka," a Godzilla-type Reptilian who claims to be the rival of Yaidron, appeared and sent hostile messages, so Yaidron tightened the security measures. This tug of war between Yaidron and Bazooka lasted until sometime around December 15.

Bazooka's UFO

Video | The reading was conducted on the spot

RYUHO OKAWA: Which planet are you from?
[*About five seconds of silence.*]

BAZOOKA: **I am the enemy of Yaidron, whom you have been contacting lately.**

INTERVIEWER A: About two weeks before former President Bush Senior passed away, he appeared in Master Ryuho Okawa's dream. Mrs. Barbara Bush was also there with Mr. Bush in the space ship, along with about 16 cows. Somehow, Master was there with them.

BAZOOKA: **You finally remembered. I abducted his soul and left his physical body where it was.**

    I sent him the precognitive dream to warn about former President Bush's death.

    I also showed him the image of cruel death of one of the cows in particular, the Awa brand cow.

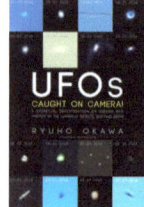

Please refer to ***UFOs Caught On Camera!*** [Tokyo: HS Press, 2018] for more information on Bazooka. Planet Elder, where Yaidron comes from, and Planet Beta, where Bazooka comes from, are considered sister planets, but Planet Beta has already been destroyed.

In the video recording, there were two other luminous objects observed. A UFO reading was conducted at a later date to investigate them.

Reading on December 13 by Edgar Cayce

"Security ship of about 8 m (26 ft.). Two of Yaidron's subordinates are on board."

Enlarged image

Video

Bazooka's UFO

Reading on December 13 by Edgar Cayce

"Security ship of about 8 m (26 ft.). Three of Yaidron's subordinates are on board."

A: Was that a declaration of war against us?

BAZOOKA: **I showed him his own end.**

RYUHO OKAWA: Look! More UFOs in the sky. Suddenly, there are more of them. Wow, one, two, three, four, five, six… There are so many of them today. (Refer to page 59, Figure 1.)

❊ ❊ ❊

RYUHO OKAWA: Who are you?

He says, "**Yaidron**."

YAIDRON: **We have contained Bazooka's actions. We will not let him harm you. You will be safe.**

Bazooka said he "abducted" Master's soul, but it was only momentarily while Master was asleep. Bazooka approached Master while his soul left his body and told him there was something to show, so Master just went along, that was all.

A: May I assume most of the people on Planet Elder share the same way of thinking as you?

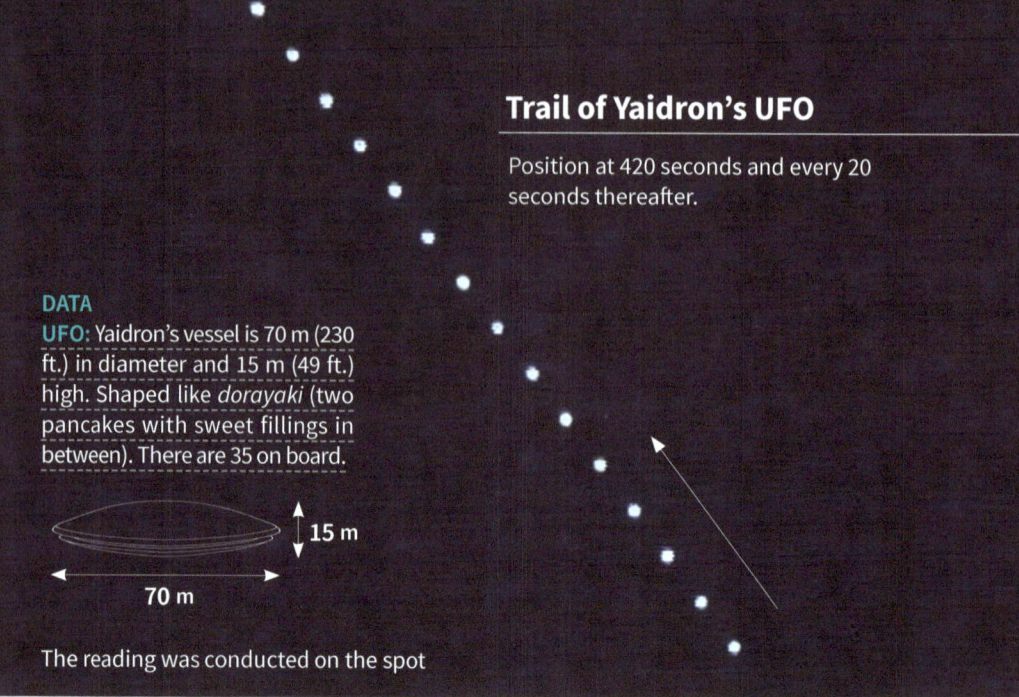

Trail of Yaidron's UFO

Position at 420 seconds and every 20 seconds thereafter.

DATA
UFO: Yaidron's vessel is 70 m (230 ft.) in diameter and 15 m (49 ft.) high. Shaped like *dorayaki* (two pancakes with sweet fillings in between). There are 35 on board.

15 m
70 m

The reading was conducted on the spot

YAIDRON: **Some people have been sent from Elder to Earth, but there are still those who remain there. I think there are some differences in how they think, but I should emphasize that we are the ones who successfully defended our planet.**

RYUHO OKAWA: It looks as if today is a battle between two fleets. There are so many UFOs.

YAIDRON: **If we must show you a fleet of UFOs, of course we will gather more of them. There are about 10 of them in the surrounding area.**

RYUHO OKAWA: Those three in a row appear to be lined up against Bazooka. (Refer to page 59, Figure 2.)

A: That is an unnatural formation.

RYUHO OKAWA: Yes, they are clearly in a defensive formation against Bazooka. [*About 10 seconds of silence.*]
    1, 2, 3, 4, 5, 6, 7, 8, 9…10. There are 10 ships.
    They are in a semicircular formation. Three of them in a row up front and two of them are positioned behind those three, then there is Yaidron.
    This is a real life "Star Wars." This is incredible. This is in fact "Star Wars."

Yaidron's security fleet formation

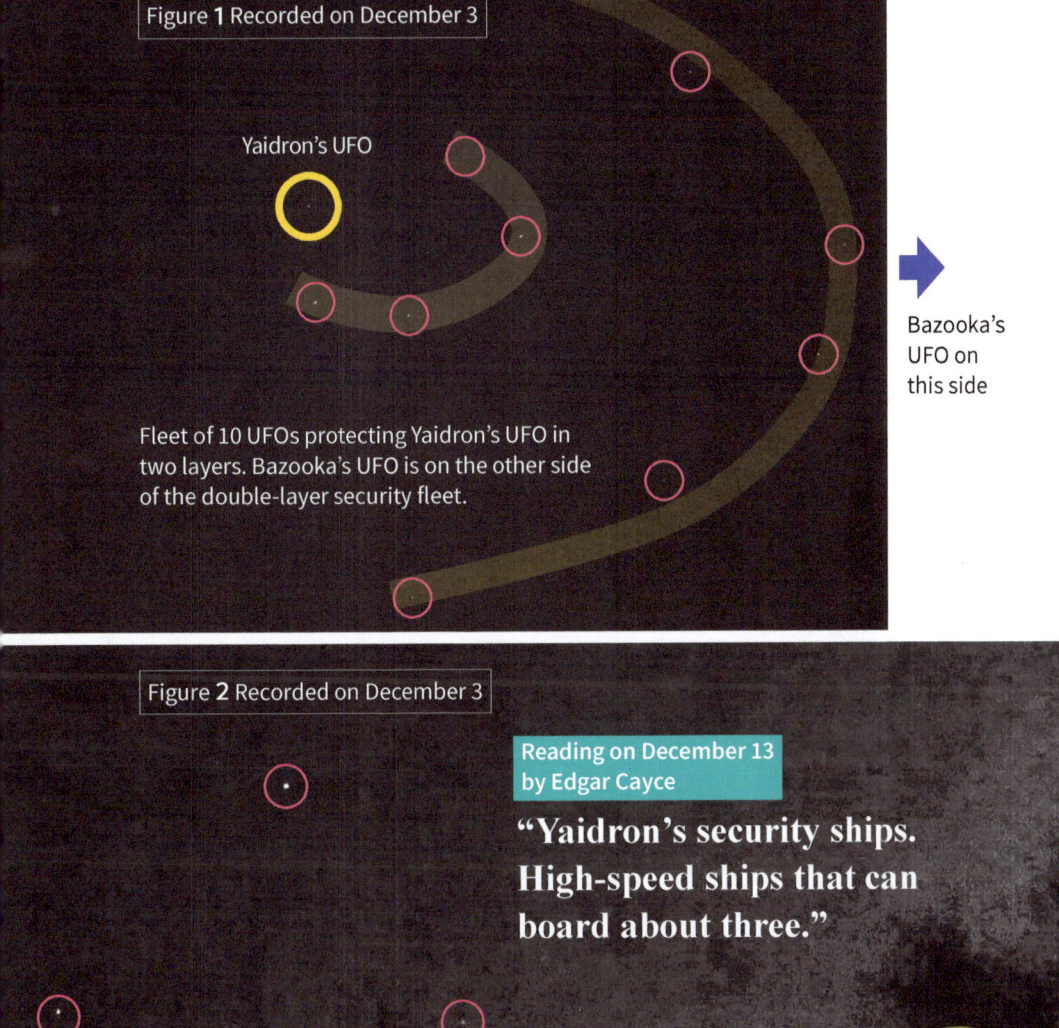

Figure 1 Recorded on December 3

Yaidron's UFO

Fleet of 10 UFOs protecting Yaidron's UFO in two layers. Bazooka's UFO is on the other side of the double-layer security fleet.

Bazooka's UFO on this side

Figure 2 Recorded on December 3

Reading on December 13 by Edgar Cayce

"Yaidron's security ships. High-speed ships that can board about three."

Bazooka's UFO was behind these leaves

In the UFO reading on December 15, an alien explained that a similar formation makes the UFO fleet look like the stars of Orion. (Refer to page 72.)

Yaidron's UFO

Reading on December 13 by Edgar Cayce

"Yaidron's fleet."

| 2018.12.8 Sat. |

Planet Elder in the Magellanic Galaxy: Yaidron 7-1 UFO Fleet

Photo

YAIDRON VS. BAZOOKA—
SPACE BATTLE ABOVE TOKYO

YAIDRON'S UFO FLEET TAKES DEFENSIVE MEASURES

| 2018.12.8 Sat. |

Planet Elder in the Magellanic Galaxy: Yaidron 7-2 UFO Fleet

Just one minute after the photo (page 61),
a security fleet of many more UFOs led by Yaidron was
photographed in another part of the sky.

Yaidron's UFO

"Two of my security ships are nearby. The others are to protect all four directions."

(Yaidron)

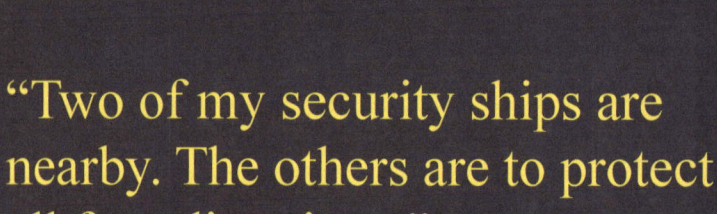

Photo | The reading was conducted on the spot

| 2018.12.13 Thu. |

Planet Elder in the Magellanic Galaxy: Yaidron 8-1 UFO Fleet

"Spiritual Messages from Amaterasu-O-Mikami On Succession of Faith" was recorded on December 13. In the same evening, more than 10 UFOs appeared.

RYUHO OKAWA: There is a fleet of UFOs all around us. They are all over the place, perhaps more than 10 of them. More than 10 of them are widely spread out.

Who is in the main luminous object? Please tell us. [*About five seconds of silence.*]

YAIDRON: This is Yaidron. There was a very important lecture today. Faith is important. It is very important.

INTERVIEWER A: Are there many of your subordinates here today?

YAIDRON: Yes, there should be more than 10 ships here. They are already widely spread out. They are all over the sky, in a formation.

They are not in tight circles, but two of my security ships are nearby. The others are keeping a certain distance to protect all four directions.

Yaidron's UFO

"Next year (2019), we must prove that the God of Earth is in fact more than just the God of Earth."

(Yaidron)

| 2018.12.13 Thu. |

Planet Elder in the Magellanic Galaxy: Yaidron 8-2 UFO Fleet

The UFO fleet taken one minute after the photo (page 64).

INTERVIEWER A: Do you have any messages for us?

YAIDRON: Next year (2019), we must prove that the God of Earth is in fact more than just the God of Earth.

He calls Himself the God of Earth, but actually, He is connected to many parts of the universe while mainly being on Earth. Earth is one of the anchors in the universe. I want to prove this next year.

El Cantare calls Himself the God of Earth, but actually, He is already becoming more than just the God of Earth. Now, He is, more and more.

DATA
UFO: Joint UFO fleet of Planet Elder and the Galactic Alliance. Yaidron's ship is pentagon-shaped with a sphere in the center.

Photo | The reading was conducted on the spot

UFO Reading on December 15

"I am honored to be guarded by space people. The other day, I had a dream that former President Bush, Mrs. Bush, and I landed on another planet along with 16 cows. This event is taken very seriously by space people. Typical ghosts (evil spirits and ikiryo) can be expelled by electric shock from UFOs."

| 2018.12.13 Thu. |

Planet Elder in the Magellanic Galaxy: Yaidron 8-3 UFO Fleet

Photo

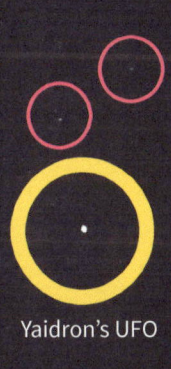

Yaidron's UFO

| 2018.12.15 Sat. |

Planet Beta in the Magellanic Galaxy: Bazooka 2

Moon

Bazooka's UFO

Video | The reading was conducted on the spot

RYUHO OKAWA: We are recording the object near the Moon now. Where did you come from? Please tell us. [*About five seconds of silence.*]
    It says, **"Too bad this is not Yaidron. I am Bazooka."**

INTERVIEWER A: Why do you keep coming to contact Master?

BAZOOKA: **Because he is too kind. He is too nice to living things.**

A: You are a living creature too, aren't you?

BAZOOKA: **I am a being beyond a living creature. You can consider me a killing machine or a creator of fear.**

A: Do you want to create fear?

BAZOOKA: **Yes. Yes. I am actually part of the principle of the universe, that is, the relationship between the ruler and the ruled. There is a principle in this universe to create a hierarchy: those who rule and those who are ruled. I am the agent of this principle.**

DATA
UFO: UFO used for monitoring. There are five on board.
The mother ship is closer to the Moon.

2018.12.15 Sat.

Planet Elder in the Magellanic Galaxy: Yaidron 9-1 UFO Fleet

"We are in position. We have deployed over 10 ships to hold their positions."
(Yaidron)

Moon

Bazooka's UFO

Photo | The reading was conducted during the video recording

RYUHO OKAWA: This luminous object is probably about 400 m (1/4 mi) above ground. Who is this? [*About five seconds of silence.*]
    It says, **"This is Yaidron, of course."**

INTERVIEWER A: Are you here because Bazooka visited us? (See page 70.)

YAIDRON: **We are in position. We have deployed over 10 ships to hold their positions. Bazooka is waiting for a chance around the year-end and New Year holidays. The current movement of Japan is the Earth Revolution. So, activities of Happy Science are extremely important.**

| 2018.12.15 Sat. |

Planet Elder in the Magellanic Galaxy: Yaidron 9-2 UFO Fleet Planet Honeykaney in Scorpius: Mycenae

RYUHO OKAWA: Where did you come from? It says it is from **"Planet Honeykaney."**

INTERVIEWER A: What is considered the important value on your planet?

MYCENAE: **We are meticulous and we like to be neat. On the other hand, we are extremely cautious. Do those stars look like Orion?**

A: Yes, they do.

MYCENAE: **Do you notice those triple stars swaying? If you look closely, they sway. They are trying to disguise themselves.**

A: Are they UFOs disguised as part of Orion?

MYCENAE: **Yes. They are not part of the constellation. They are faking themselves to look like they are part of Orion. We outnumber Bazooka right now, so there is nothing to worry about. There are over a dozen ships on standby in the sky.**

A: I think you are also protecting the Lord on Earth. Among all the teachings of Master, which part are you drawn to the most?

MYCENAE: **Kindness. I think being kind is very important. Bazooka is wrong. Kindness is a value we must protect. It is one of the attributes of God.**

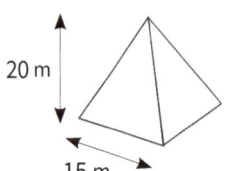

DATA
Alien: Looks like a tabby cat standing upright. About 120 cm (3 ft. 11 in.). They have a pouch on their abdomen. Unisex (closer to female).
UFO: Pyramid-shaped, 20 m (65 ft.) high and 15 m (50 ft.) wide at the base. There are 13 on board.

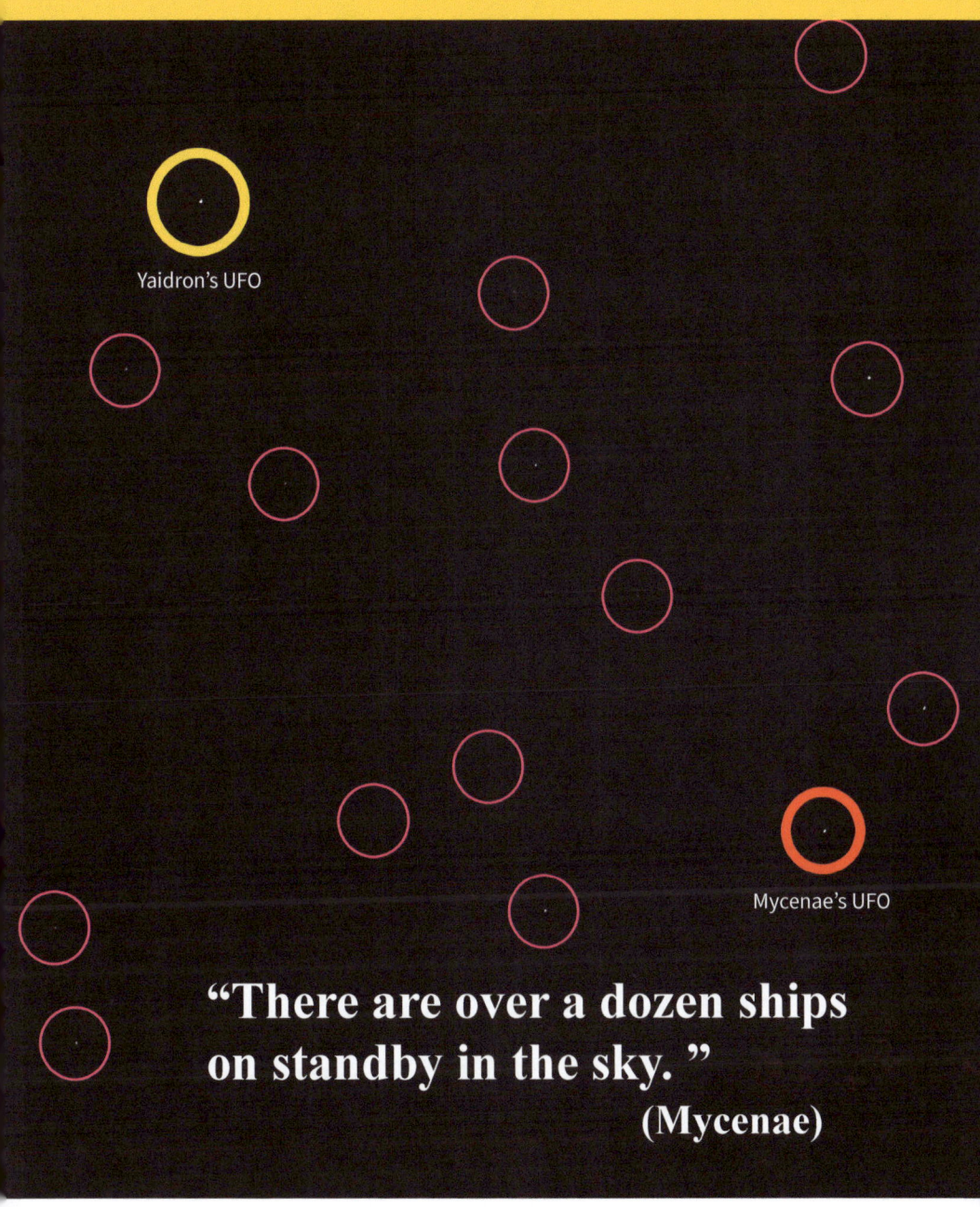

Photo | The reading was conducted during the video recording

| 2018.12.19 Wed. |

Andromeda Galaxy

RYUHO OKAWA: If there is a lifeform on board, I would like to speak to you. [*About five seconds of silence.*]
    It is laughing, **"Ha, ha, ha!"**

INTERVIEWER A: Are you a male or a female?

ALIEN FROM ANDROMEDA GALAXY: I am a man.

A: What do you look like?

ALIEN FROM ANDROMEDA GALAXY: Oh, I look like "Baikin-man (a Japanese anime character)." You can imagine Baikin-man on his toy UFO.

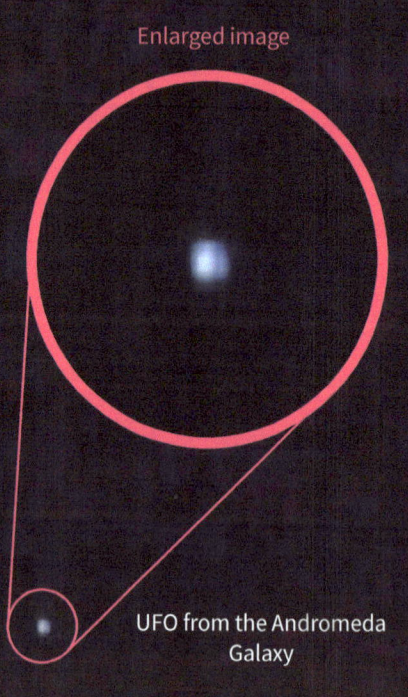

Enlarged image

UFO from the Andromeda Galaxy

DATA
Alien: Resembles the anime character Baikin-man.
UFO: About 7 m (23 ft.) wide and 2.5 m (8 ft.) high. It looks like two ashtrays put together.

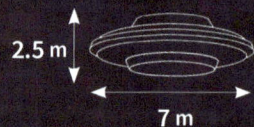

2.5 m

7 m

| 2018.12.19 Wed. |

Planet Southern: White

In the video recording of the UFO from the Andromeda Galaxy, another luminous object was observed. A UFO reading was conducted at a later date to investigate the object.

Reading on December 30 by Rient Arl Croud

"Planet Southern UFO, leader: 'White.' White hair, goatee, age unknown. It can board three. Looks like a Japanese-style top. Small-sized vessel, 12 m (39 ft.) × 3 m (10 ft.)"

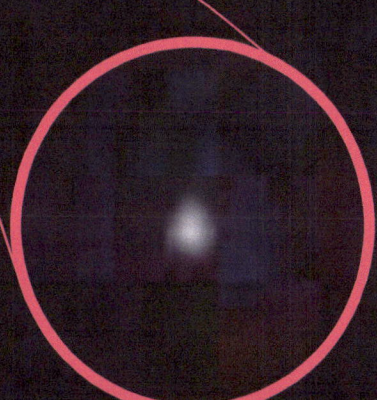

Enlarged image

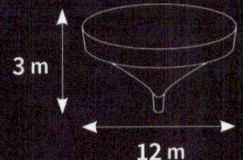

3 m
12 m

Video | The reading was conducted on the spot

2018.12.19 Wed.

Planet Migel in Delphinus: McCartney 3-1

RYUHO OKAWA: Do you have anything you want to say? [*About 10 seconds of silence.*]

MCCARTNEY: You need more heroes with burning passion. I am working on strengthening and increasing powers for heroes. In fact, there are musicians among the heroes. So, I must guide them.

Master Ryuho Okawa will be creating more and more music, so I am visiting every so often to pave a path in that direction. You want to spread sensational music all around the Earth, the world, so I believe you will need greater inspiration for that.

Video | The reading was conducted on the spot

DATA
UFO: Square box-shaped bottom with a saturno hat on top.

McCartney's UFO

2018.12.19 Wed.

Planet Santhor

Enlarged image

In the video recording of McCartney's UFO, another luminous object was observed. A UFO reading was conducted at a later date to investigate the object.

Reading on December 30 by Rient Arl Croud

"UFO from Planet Santhor near Orihime in the Milky Way. Four oriental females. Chinese, Korean, Japanese, and Thai. It is 15 m (49 ft.) × 4 m (13 ft.)"

| 2018.12.19 Wed. |

Planet Migel in Delphinus: McCartney 3-2 UFO Fleet

Photo

In the video recording of UFO from Planet Migel in Delphinus (pages 76 ~ 77), other luminous objects were observed. A UFO reading was conducted at a later date to investigate the objects.

Reading on December 30 by Rient Arl Croud

"I think they are the usual members."

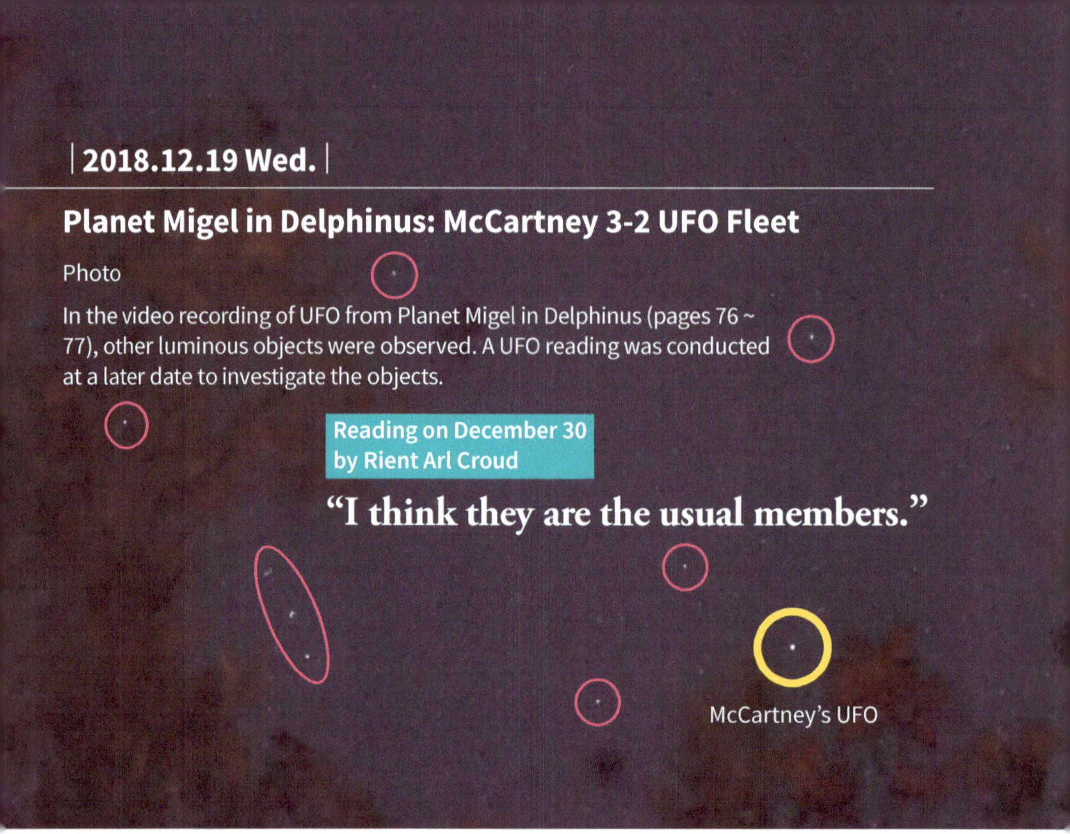

McCartney's UFO

| 2018.12.27 Thu. |

From the Mother Ship near Venus

Photo

Reading on December 30 by Rient Arl Croud

"You can see those as usual three stars with the naked eye. Zooming in, two of them split vertically into two saucers each, so they are not stars. The UFOs came from the mother ship near Venus. They came to observe the holiday season from Christmas to the end of the year.

By remote-viewing, a kappa (Japanese water imp)-like cyborg was observed. Maybe it is for research purposes."

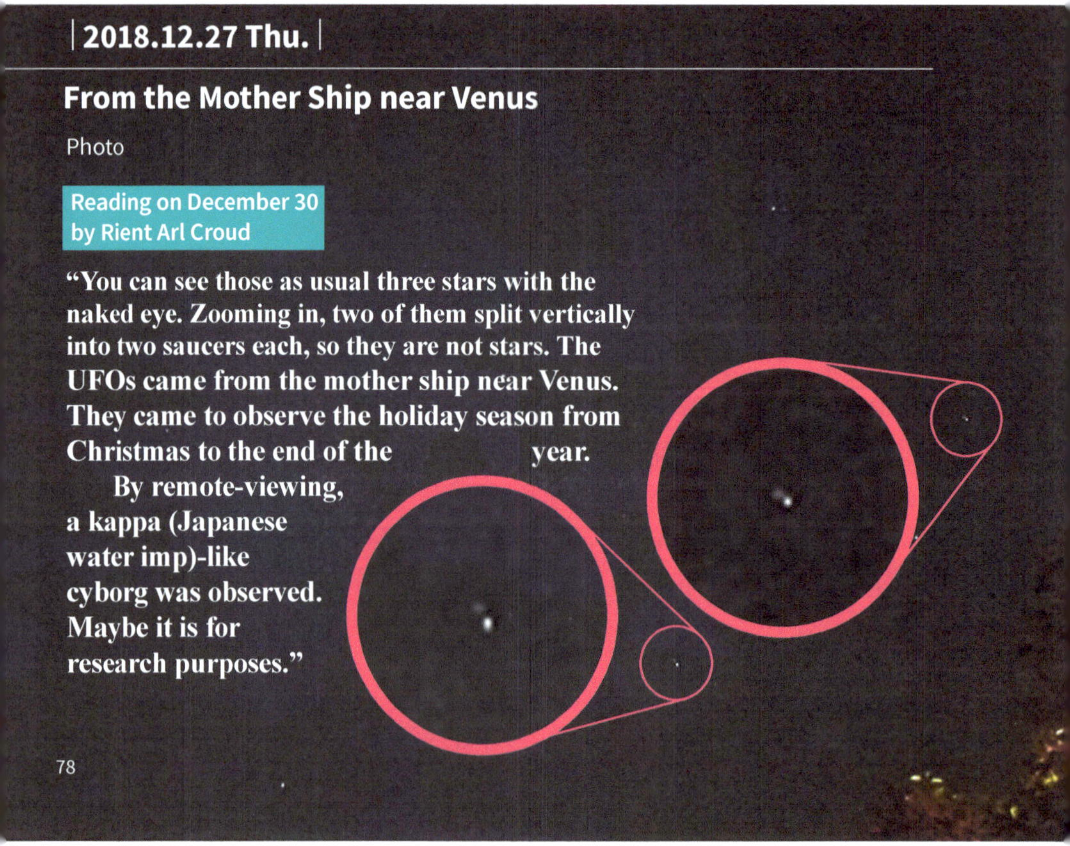

| 2018.12.27 Thu. |

Planet Mohican in Capricornus: New Yorker

Video | The reading was conducted on the spot

RYUHO OKAWA: There are more than 17, 18, or maybe over 20 luminous objects in the sky. I am curious about the one right above us. Let me try to communicate with it.

NEW YORKER: **Our planet is very advanced in weaving technology. People on Earth have benefited from our technology. Earth's textile industry improved since the technology from Planet Mohican in Capricornus was brought in.**

INTERVIEWER A: What do you look like?

NEW YORKER: **On our planet, we put a lot of emphasis on clothing, so we are wearing many different types of fashion.**

A: Is there a particular reason why you chose to appear today?

NEW YORKER: **Actually, we take turns visiting. Yaidron is not here today. He may be doing something else.**

DATA
Alien: Resembles human face with flaxen hair. Male.
UFO: Top part is shaped like a pointy hat. Bottom part is round and spotted like a poisonous mushroom. There are 36 on board.

2018.12.28 Fri.

Planet Elder in the Magellanic Galaxy: Yaidron 10

Video | The reading was conducted on the spot

RYUHO OKAWA: That UFO has not moved since we saw it earlier. If it is a star, it should have moved by now. Whose UFO are we looking at?

YAIDRON: This is Yaidron. I am sorry I was away from last night until this afternoon. I went to Okinawa to inspect the area.

INTERVIEWER A: On the camera, it looks like you are moving down very fast. (See the picture on page 81.)

YAIDRON: I see. It appears that way to you.
　　You have proofread "Spiritual Messages from Mao Zedong" this morning, and this afternoon, you were attacked by his spirit. I suggested you record spiritual messages from Mao Zedong, so it is clear I am his enemy. Unless you strike and defeat him, it won't be enough. Just striking Xi Jinping alone will not destroy China.

You must target Kim Il Sung of North Korea and Mao Zedong of China, too. As long as people are treating Mao Zedong as a good man, you won't be able to bring China down.

A: After WWII, during the Clinton administration, the U.S. supported China more than they did Japan. They are guilty of turning China into a giant that it is now.

YAIDRON: Yes, they must reflect on what they have done. Especially considering what China has been doing.
Master Ryuho Okawa had researched about Hannah Arendt while he was still a student and studied the origin of totalitarianism. So, you can consider this movement as his lifework. It is your great mission to pulverize the next big crime of their totalitarianism.
In the year 2019, we must change the course of China's destiny largely including the fate of Uyghur, Mongolia, and Tibet. I am determined to do so and I will sink Bazooka for sure. He has shown up now. I think he has connections to the current political leaders of China. He might be sending inspiration to them.

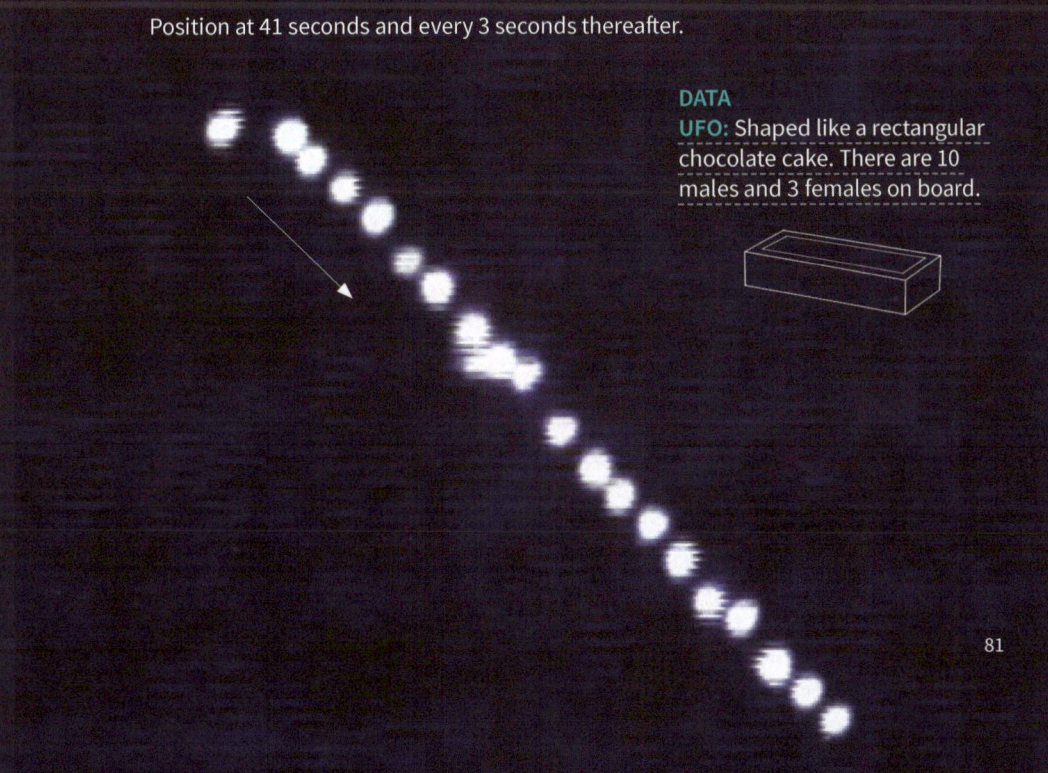

| 2018.12.28 Fri. |

Planet Needle in Cancer/Andromeda Galaxy

Enlarged image

Enlarged image

UFO from Andromeda Galaxy

Video | The reading was conducted on the spot

UFO from Planet Needle

RYUHO OKAWA: [*Talking toward the UFO*] Can you talk to me? The one on the camera says it is from **"Planet Needle."** This is the first one from there.

INTERVIEWER A: Are you a male or female?

ALIEN FROM PLANET NEEDLE: Female.

A: What do you look like?

ALIEN FROM PLANET NEEDLE: I am wearing a red skin-tight battle suit. I have noticeable ears, not horns. I have brown hair, large cat-like eyes, and a whip in my hand.

A: Why did you come here?

ALIEN FROM PLANET NEEDLE:
To study and observe.

RYUHO OKAWA: Now, there is another UFO. The one to the upper left of the UFO from Planet Needle, can you speak to us? [*About five seconds of silence.*] **"Andromeda?"**

ALIEN FROM ANDROMEDA GALAXY:
Greetings for the coming new year.

A: I see. Please have a nice new year.

DATA (PLANET NEEDLE)
Alien: Female in a red battle suit. Brown hair, with ears protruding diagonally like a cat's. Large, cat-like eyes. *Neko-musume* (Japanese anime character) style.
UFO: It can board a single passenger.

Part 3

January – May 2019

The Battle between Light and Darkness

Into the Age of Cosmic-Scale Truth

From now on, you will face new challenges or arguments that you have never thought of.

For example, in past wars, people had been fighting over justice that was confined to Earth. Since ancient times, people have continued to struggle for supremacy on Earth to decide which side is right.

However, now human beings are about to step into the world beyond that.

Humanity has entered the Space Age. We have entered the age when people begin to ask what the justice or the Truth of the space age is.

When I think about the prospects of 2,000 or 3,000 years into the future from the 21st century, we must take the enlightenment about the universe, the Truth or justice of Space Age into consideration. You will make a mistake if you make a judgment based only on the past Truth or justice.

From *The Contact*

| 2019.1.1 Tue. |

Planet Include in Sagittarius: Metatron, Yamoozay (Yamrozay) 1

RYUHO OKAWA: I just have received a message (from UFO) that they **"have a connection with Jesus Christ,"** so I am now taking the video with my staff.

Please ask if you have any questions. I'll begin communicating with them.

INTERVIEWER A: Are you Jesus Christ?

METATRON: **No. Jesus Christ himself is not a space being. Jesus is one of great spirits on Earth, but he is originally from Sagittarius. He is part of the soul called Amor.**

A: Does your planet have a name?

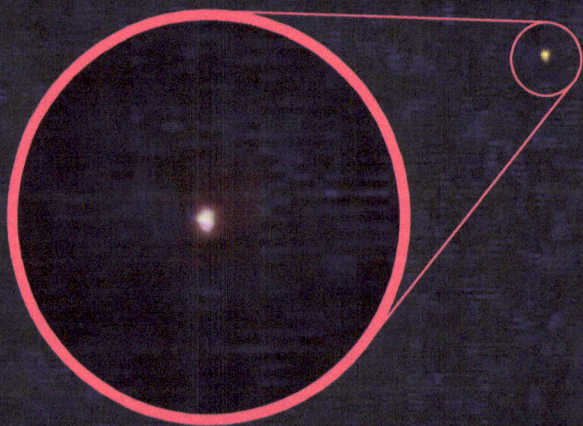

Enlarged image

Video | The reading was conducted on the spot

METATRON: **Planet Include in Sagittarius. My name is…Metatron.**
I have been watching over Christian people who have been working hard on Earth, from outer space. Now, Happy Science is giving out most strongly the light of love that is one of attributes of Jesus Christ, so I am trying to help you.

A: What brought you here today?

METATRON: **Well, I think I should make a new year's greetings.**
Christian countries are still advanced countries, so Happy Science will not be able to be influential unless its teachings spread further in advanced countries. So, we want to convey to them, "Jesus Christ and his soul siblings are directly guiding Happy Science and sending our messages through Master Okawa."

A: How many people can your UFO hold?

METATRON: **There are only two people on board [*laughs*].**

A: What kind of people are on board?

METATRON: **My wife.**

RYUHO OKAWA: He calls her **"Yamoozay (short for Yamrozay)."**

A: Do you have any messages for us?

METATRON: We will work hard to make this year a year of love and peace. Your name will become known around the world this year. I predict this and want to help you to realize this.

Photo shows the color and location of the luminous object at 130 seconds and every 3 seconds thereafter.

DATA
Alien (Metatron): He has a goat-like face. He stands on two legs. He is about 220 cm (7 ft. 3 in.) tall. He is wearing a white lacy uniform and laced boots.
Alien (Yamrozay): She is about 175 cm (5 ft. 9 in.) tall. She wears something like an ancient Greek or Egyptian long robe.
UFO: It looks like a globe with a ring like Saturn's ring around it. It is 8 m (26.4 ft.) in diameter and 3 m (9.9 ft.) high. There is a mother ship at an altitude of 10,000 to 20,000 meters.

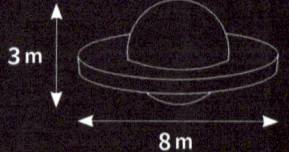

Metatron—the space soul of Jesus Christ who supports El Cantare

Metatron is a seraph (the highest rank of angel who protects El Cantare) and one of the Gods of Light. He is one of the consciousnesses of Amor, Jesus Christ's space soul. When there were big wars occurring on Earth, he had helped earthlings restore peace as a symbolic figure that represents cosmic power.

It is said that about 6,500 years ago, he was born in Mesopotamia. Now he is supporting El Cantare who descended on Earth as Ryuho Okawa.

Since January 2019, Metatron has given us many spiritual messages.

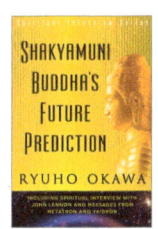 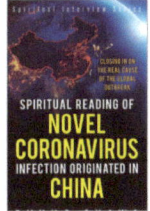

These two books partly include UFO readings in which Metatron talks about the novel coronavirus.
Shakyamuni Buddha's Future Prediction [Tokyo: HS Press, 2020] (left)
Spiritual Reading of Novel Coronavirus Infection Originated in China [Tokyo: HS Press, 2020] (right)

| 2019.1.2 Wed. |

Planet Nix in the Small Magellanic Cloud: Liu Bei 5

Liu Bei's UFO

RYUHO OKAWA: A luminous flying object, do you have something to say? [*About five seconds of silence.*]

LIU BEI: Yes. I am Liu Bei from the star cluster that supports you. I came to greet you on the second day of the new year.

INTERVIEWER A: Planet Nix! Thank you. We are very happy to hear that. Are you still in Germany?

LIU BEI: No, I'm moving quite a lot now.
   I have quite a lot of secret missions. I cannot tell you all of them. There is something like Ninja diplomacy.

A: On Planet Nix, what kind of values do you consider important?

LIU BEI: On Planet Nix, it is important for us to help others without being noticed.

A: Do you all have a human-like appearance?

LIU BEI: Umm… I cannot say we all are, but you could think we have a human-like appearance as it is difficult to explain.

DATA
UFO: The classic Adamski-type UFO.
It can hold three people.

Video | The reading was conducted on the spot

| 2019.1.2 Wed. |

Planet Inuyasha in Cassiopeia

The reading was conducted at a later date because another luminous object was projected in the video.

Enlarged image

UFO reading on January 10 by Rient Arl Croud

"Aliens have a zombie-like appearance.
Their UFO can hold five people.
A top-shaped UFO, 15 m (49.5 ft.) in diameter and 5 m (16.5 ft.) thick.
Aliens resembling Inuyasha from Cassiopeia.
(Inuyasha might be a character in a Japanese manga series?)
They have a mysterious ability to restore their original shape even if they are slashed into pieces."

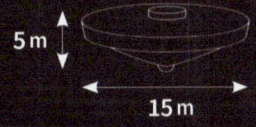
5 m
15 m

| 2019.1.2 Wed. |

The Fourth Planet of Pleiades (Planet Sachertorte)

RYUHO OKAWA: The UFO was witnessed sometime in the evening on January 2. I think it came to send us some New Year's message. [*About 20 seconds of silence.*]

ALIEN FROM SACHERTORTE: **Umm… We started renaissance in Austria.**

Our planet has a close connection to Pleiades. I think it is the Fourth planet of Pleiades. Chocolate was invented on our planet. It is the planet of chocolate.

Among earthlings' culture, you are yet to be revealed where in the universe chocolate or cakes came from. There must be someone who invented them somewhere in the universe.

Video
UFO Reading on January 3

DATA
UFO: The decorated cake-type. There are 20 people on board.

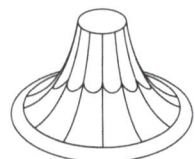

| 2019.1.14 Mon. |

Planet Southern: Mille-feuille

The reading was conducted at a later date because another luminous object was included in the video of McCartney's UFO (p.93).

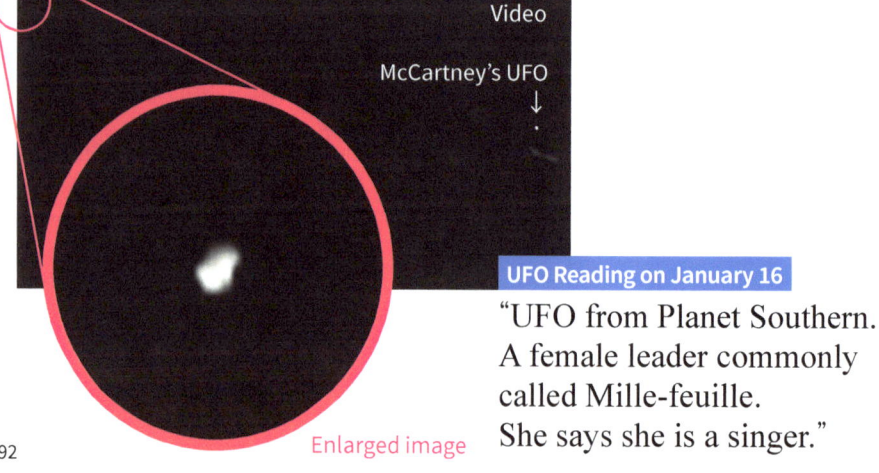

Video
McCartney's UFO ↓

UFO Reading on January 16

"UFO from Planet Southern. A female leader commonly called Mille-feuille. She says she is a singer."

Enlarged image

| 2019.1.14 Mon. |

Planet Miguel in Delphinus: McCartney 4

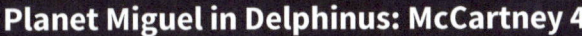

Photo shows the color and location of the luminous flying object at 203 seconds and every 5 seconds thereafter.

Video | The reading was conducted on the spot

INTERVIEWER A: Was some power from universe working on the Beatles?

MCCARTNEY: Obviously. The fact that we became popular throughout the world shows some energy from the universe was working on us.

A: Do you have a message for us today?

MCCARTNEY: Hundreds of millions of believers should be one of your objectives. At least, hundreds of millions of people should be influenced by Happy Science by listening to lectures or reading books. You have to get to the point where hundreds of millions of people directly learn your teachings and the rest of the world indirectly know them.

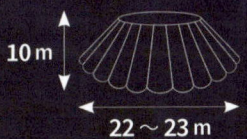

DATA
Alien with long, flaxen hair
UFO: Shaped like a pleated skirt (Mt. Fuji-shaped or pudding-shaped).
It is about 22 ~ 23 m (72.6 ~ 75.9 ft.) in diameter and 10 m (33 ft.) high.
It can hold 30 people.

| 2019.1.17 Thu. |

Planet Michaeta in Pisces: Iktron
Planet Engel in Pisces: Goeppels 2

INTERVIEWER A: What values do you consider important in Pisces?

IKTRON: People in Pisces like fortune-telling very much [*laughs*]. To tell the truth, we like future prediction so much that we don't know whether we should call it studying or playing. That is what we are doing. We specialize in future prediction.

I sense that you will be facing problems both at home and abroad.

That is why you need a good leader. So, you should not get discouraged, but you must work harder bearing in mind that Ryuho Okawa still has a mission to fulfill.

Iktron's UFO

DATA
Alien: Looks like a buffalo and is standing on two legs. He is wearing a space suit. Male.
UFO: It looks like a combination of two trapezoids folded into a circle. It is 20 m (66 ft.) long and several meters high. Seven people are on board.

20 m

Video | The reading was conducted on the spot

UFO Reading on January 23 by Yaidron

"☆Yaidron's explanation
UFO from Planet Engel in Pisces (we met in Germany).

It was investigating the whole Japan on the day when the Great Hanshin Earthquake occurred."

Another luminous object was included in the video, so the reading was conducted at a later date.

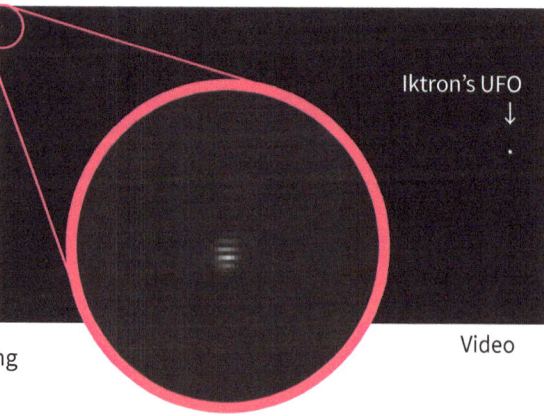

Goeppels' UFO

| 2019.1.23 Wed. |

Planet Elder in Magellanic Galaxy: Yaidron 11

INTERVIEWER A : Thank you as always for your help.

YAIDRON: **We are here to try to cheer you up.**
I am sure you are all discouraged because your movie, *The Laws of the Universe-Part I* **was not nominated for Academy Award for Best Animated Feature.**
We, your space friends, are actually all discouraged.
The movie had received Special Jury Animation Award at the Awareness Film Festival in Los Angeles, so we thought it most likely received an Academy Award.

A: We sincerely appreciate your support.

YAIDRON: **But you are ready to make the second and the third movie, and Ms. Sayaka Okawa is writing the script of the next film,** *The Laws of the Universe - The Age of Elohim*, **which I believe will be much better. And they may be able to prepare earlier.**
We aren't giving up yet. We are also guardians of humankind on Earth. We have been watching over you as guardians of humankind, passing the baton to our successors for a long time.

Video | The reading was conducted on the spot

2019 Late February | Taipei

Master's missionary tour in Taiwan

Having visited Germany in October 2018, Master Ryuho Okawa set out on his missionary tour in Taiwan in late February 2019. He gave a lecture titled, "Love Surpasses Hatred" in Taipei on March 3. He offered us a guide for protecting freedom and democracy in Taiwan as well as peace in Asia from China, a totalitarian nation. The UFO reading conducted after returning to Japan revealed that many space people supported him in his missionary tour in Taiwan.

The lecture in Master's missionary tour in Taiwan on March 3, 2019

"Love Surpasses Hatred"

（以愛跨超憎恨）At Grand Hyatt Taipei

Please choose political systems that will bring people happiness, not suffering. I clearly want to say that the people of a nation hold the responsibility, duty, and the right to create and construct such systems.

- From Chapter Three, "Love Surpasses Hatred" in *Love for the Future* [New York: IRH Press, 2019]

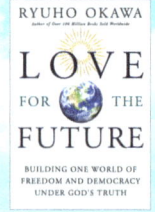

Space people who supported Master in his missionary tour in Taiwan

I gave a lecture titled, "Love Surpasses Hatred" in Taiwan on March 3 this year. Before the departure, Metatron came to tell me that he would be responsible for guarding me for a week before and after my missionary tour in Taiwan, which felt strange to me. […]

And I gave a lecture, "Love Surpasses Hatred" in a hotel where lots of people from Taiwan and China came. Only on that day, I felt that Metatron came down to me along with Jesus Christ who was supposed to be the assistant spirit of the lecture.

At that time, I felt he came down to me out of concern that Jesus might not have enough power.

From the introductory comment of
"Spiritual Messages from Metatron"
Recorded on March 21, 2019

The streets of Taipei, Taiwan. The bamboo-shaped skyscraper Taipei 101 is known as a sightseeing spot.

| 2019.3.4 Mon. | Taipei |

Dragon-shaped clouds

During the journey from Tanshui to Taipei on the day after the lecture, images of dragon-shaped clouds were taken.

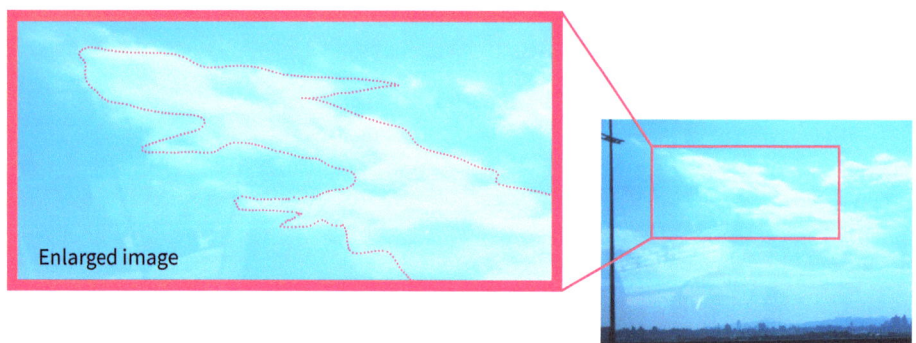

"Dragon-shaped clouds were seen" (Photos above)

"The clouds looked like a dragon sleeping over the mountain" (Photo below)

Members of the Galactic Federation all have agreed that we should thwart the flip-side universe's plan to invade Earth through the People's Republic of China.

The power from the universe is at work. So, we hope you will be able to receive the power. Now, we are fighting the real enemy.

That is why dragons are protecting Taiwan.

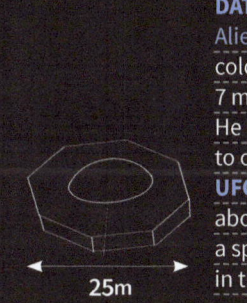

DATA
Alien: He looks like a colorful small dragon about 7 m long. Male.
He uses collaborative robots to operate machines.
UFO: Octagon-shaped, about 25 m in diameter with a spherical area protruding in the center.

Video | The reading was conducted on the spot

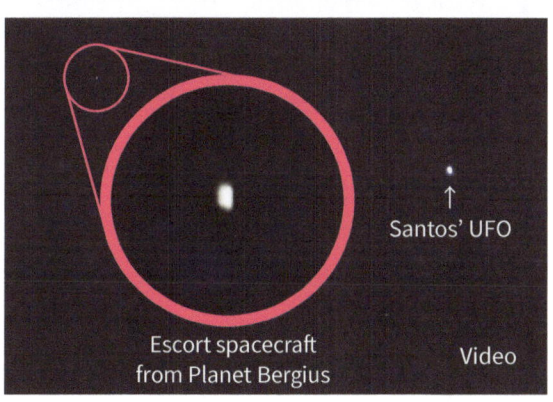

An additional reading was conducted two days later because another luminous object was included in the video of Santos' UFO.

The UFO reading on March 9 by Santos

"He (Santos) says that this is an escort spacecraft of the main UFO (for three people) from Bergius."

| 2019.3.8 Fri. |

Planet Elder in Magellanic Galaxy: Yaidron 12

Video | The reading was conducted on the spot

YAIDRON: **I am back from Taiwan. I'll go back to normal duties.**

INTERVIEWER A: All right. Thank you.

YAIDRON: **Happy Science is doing various things, but each effort has not come to fruition. It is just sowing seeds, but not spreading its teachings enough. After all, it lacks the power to start a revolution.**
   But this year (2019), we will work hard to make this year a year of miracle. We want to make clear what is good and what is evil, what is heavenly and what is hellish, or what is the front-side universe and what is the flip-side universe. So, please have a strong mind.

A: Look, there are three luminous objects. To the left side of the condominium. (Refer to the lower photo on page 101)

YAIDRON: **Yes. They are small spacecraft. They are escort spacecraft, so to speak.**

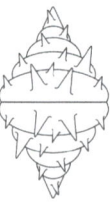

DATA
UFO: It is shaped like two turban shells combined. It has five stories each, above and below. It is rotating and changing its color.

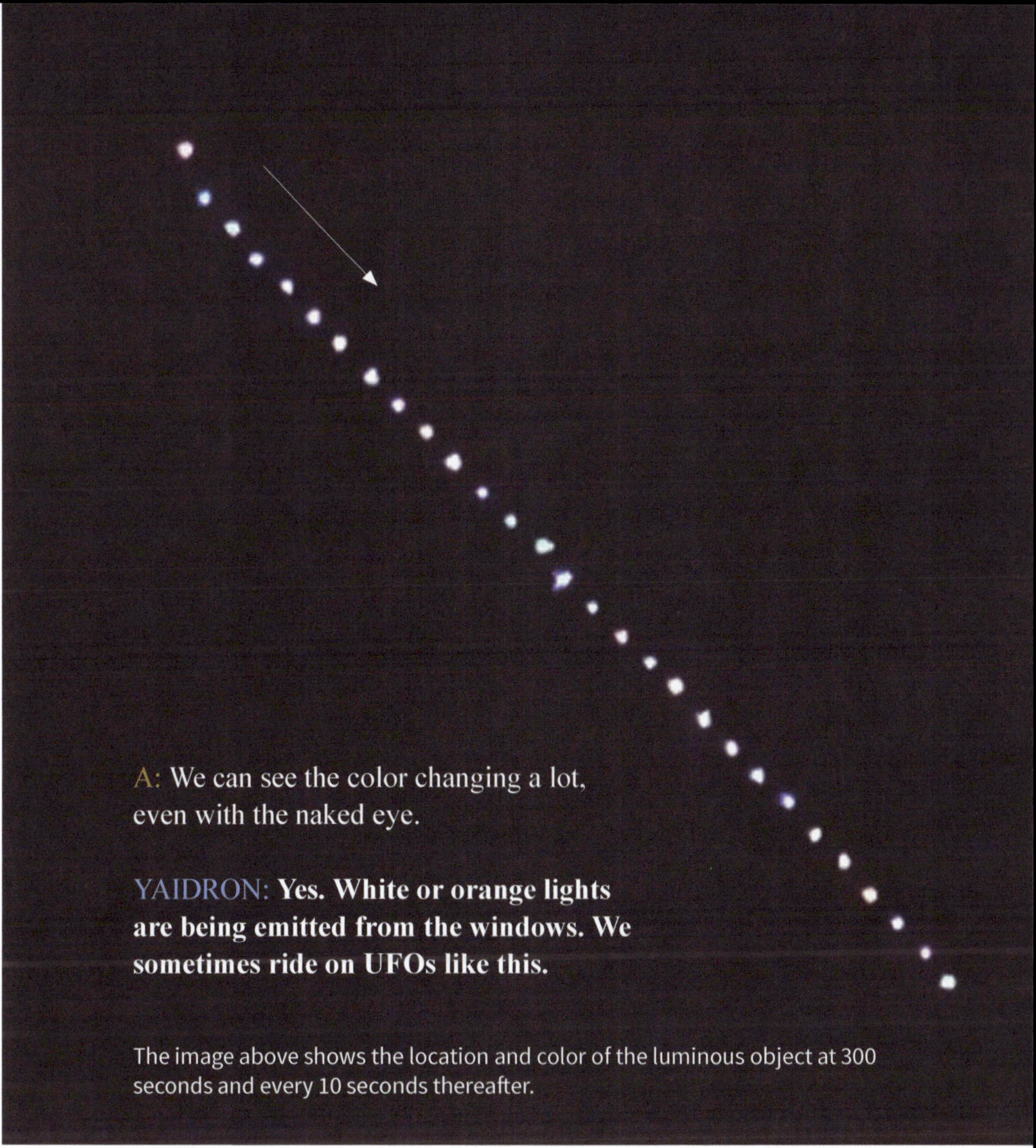

A: We can see the color changing a lot, even with the naked eye.

YAIDRON: **Yes. White or orange lights are being emitted from the windows. We sometimes ride on UFOs like this.**

The image above shows the location and color of the luminous object at 300 seconds and every 10 seconds thereafter.

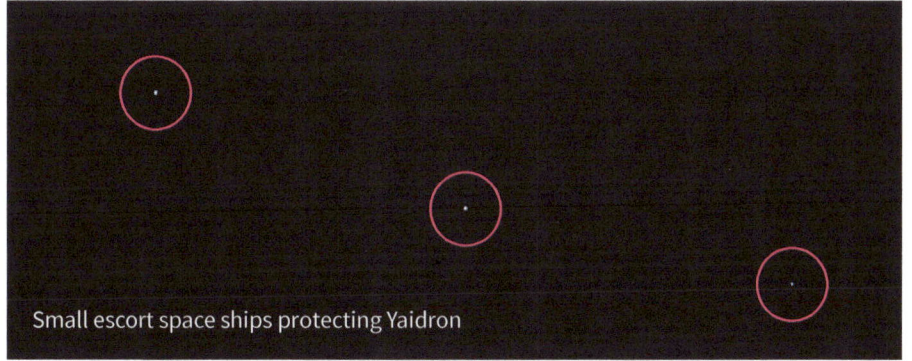

Small escort space ships protecting Yaidron

| 2019.3.21 Thu. |

Planet Include in Sagittarius: Metatron, Yamrozay 2

Video | The reading was conducted on the spot

RYUHO OKAWA: We recorded the spiritual messages from Metatron in the morning hours.

Looking at it from the balcony, we can see the object that is emitting a brilliant light and it looks as if it is sending a signal. I think it wants to talk further about the previous topic.

METATRON: **Of course, this is the UFO from Planet Include. Metatron, Yamrozay, and others came here because you called us.**

Planet Include actually does not have the same system of reincarnation as Earth.

It is also known as "Planet of Messiah." People on Planet Include have already broken free of the cycle of reincarnation. They are allowed to materialize themselves from the heavenly world and return there afterwards. This requires some level of certification.

One of the points that I did not mention today was about LGBT. We are deeply concerned about it and are investigating whether it can be considered true love.

INTERVIEWER A: Ms. Yamrozay, do you have any messages for us?

| 2019.3.21 Thu. |

Planet Include in Sagittarius: Saitron, Semrozay

The readings were conducted at a later date because some luminous objects were included in the video of the UFO of Metatron and Yamrozay.

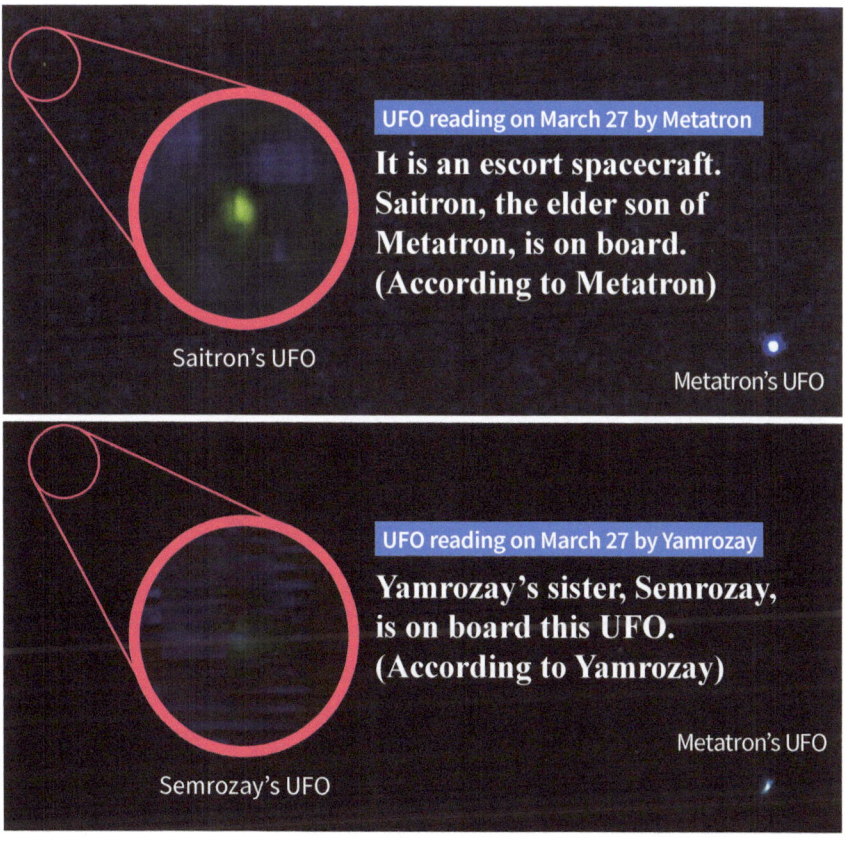

Video

YAMROZAY: **You are getting involved in the show business, so I want to cast some light to support you.**

A: I hear that you have a healing power.

YAMROZAY: **Yes, I have a healing power. But art itself has a healing power.**
   Art has the power to purify the mind or soul of people and make them happy. This is what we are studying.

| 2019.3.24 Sun. |

The Third Star (γ) in Bergius: Nichaetatron and Others

Video | The reading was conducted on the spot

RYUHO OKAWA: It is trying to send a message by flickering. Who are you? [*About five seconds of silence.*] It says, **"Nichaetatron."**

INTERVIEWER A: What planet are you from?

NICHAETATRON: We come from a companion star of Bergius. You can call it Bergius γ.

A: You have "tron" in your name. Mr. Metatron often comes to us. Are you on his side?

NICHAETATRON: Yes. Those who have "tron" in their names are usually friends. It means "the one who gives light" on each planet.

A: What kind of teachings or thoughts do people in Bergius γ value?

NICHAETATRON: We are now aiming to become the source of light. We are studying about "how should the light be in the universe?" In our terms, to become the light means to be enlightened.

DATA
Alien: A male alien who looks like a human. About 180cm (5 ft. 11 in.) tall. He can disappear and travel by breaking himself down into photons. He is good at healing.
UFO: 12 people are on board.

The reading was conducted at a later date because four luminous objects were included in the video of Nichaetatron's UFO.

UFO reading on March 27 by Rient Arl Croud

"Three female aliens from the Seventh Planet 'Mew' in Lyra"

"Aliens called 'Thoughtful' who came from the Fourth Planet in the Pleiades (They insist they are not only superficial but people of substance). A total of four aliens: two males and two females."

Video

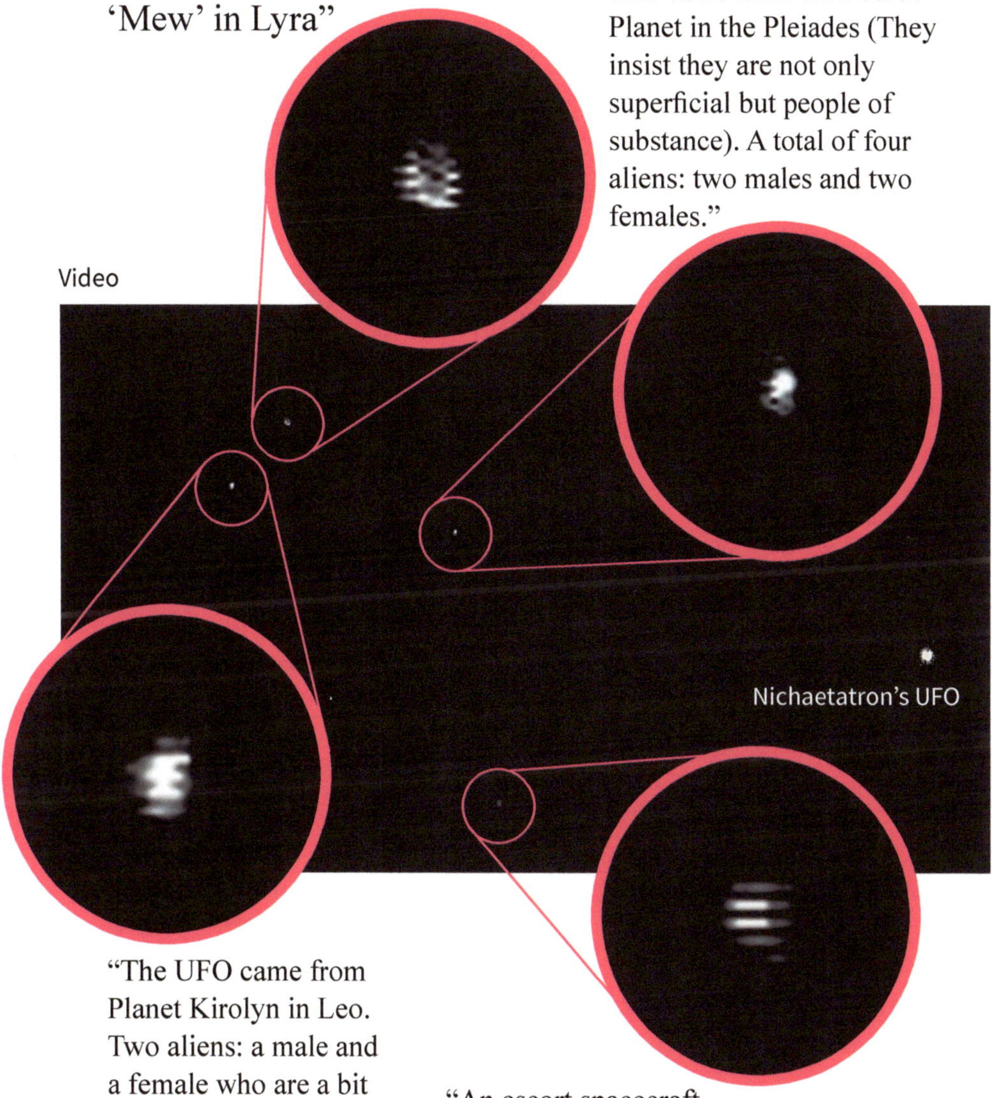

Nichaetatron's UFO

"The UFO came from Planet Kirolyn in Leo. Two aliens: a male and a female who are a bit herbivorous."

"An escort spacecraft from the Third Star of Bergius. Three battle-type Greys are on board."

105

| 2019.3.24 Sun. |

Planet Pixel in Andromeda Galaxy: Tortootsie (Angulimala)

Aide to Master Shio Okawa gave a lecture about a picture book titled, *The Tale of Village Chief Miracle ~The Spider's Thread~*. On that night, a UFO with space people on board appeared in response to it.

Video | The reading was conducted on the spot

RYUHO OKAWA: The one who drove away Nichaetatron and came into camera view, who are you?

TORTOOTSIE: **I am called Angulimala in Buddhism. That story was about a Reptilian who devoted himself to Buddha's teachings.**

INTERVIEWER A: Thanks to your anecdote, we can learn lots of important things.

TORTOOTSIE: **Right. We were listening to today's lecture on The Spider's Thread while flying, and we want you to tell the story of Angulimala. Please.**
  What about the story of Buddha's divine power and the conversion of the one who is about to commit murder? Please do publish the book.

DATA
Alien: Pterosaur-type alien
UFO: Hamburger-shaped UFO with three people on board

| 2019.4.27 Sat. |

Orion: Amemiko

Video | The reading was conducted on the spot

RYUHO OKAWA: It says **"We came from Orion."**

INTERVIEWER A: What message does it have for us?

RYUHO OKAWA: It says **"We came from New York."** It also says, **"What a nominee for the Federal Reserve Board of Governors in New York is saying is correct."**

A: Are you an alien who has a connection to Mr. Stephen Moore?

AMEMIKO: **Yes. I am the one who is watching over the finance-related matters in the U.S.**

We are planning on getting Japan and the U.S. to unite and thwart Beijing's bid for financial supremacy.

We are going to destroy the One Belt One Road initiative by cutting off the financial sources. Our key strategy is to destroy credit in China.

We are now thinking about causing a financial crisis comparable to Lehman shock in China. We are now even simulating what will happen after that.

DATA
Alien: A male alien standing on two legs with folds on them.
His head is shaped like a bowl and he has giant scissors for his hands.
UFO: It has lights on the tip of its top and bottom parts. The middle part is on invisible mode. Five people are on board.

2019.4.27 Sat.

The Pleiades: Maitreya

A UFO with space people on board was witnessed on the night Master gave a lecture titled, "The Strength to Protect Faith" at Sohonzan (Head Temple) Shoshinkan of Happy Science (Utsunomiya, Tochigi Pref.).

Video | The reading was conducted on the spot

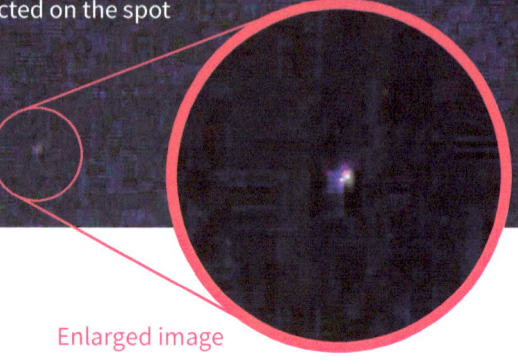

Enlarged image

RYUHO OKAWA: Really? It is calling itself **"Maitreya."** It says, **"I am Maitreya who is guiding you from outer space."**

INTERVIEWER A: What brought it here today?

RYUHO OKAWA: It says it came from Utsunomiya today.

A: Then, was it protecting us?

MAITREYA: **We were in the sky above (Shoshinkan) and broadcasting the lecture live to our planet.**

　Our mission has been revealed. Master has politically revealed our mission to fight with those who are drawing spiritual energy from the dark side universe, which I am sure will raise everyone's spirit.

A: Where did you come from?

MAITREYA: **Now, we are using Venus as our base, but many of us are goddesses who originally came from the Pleiades.**

　We are now guiding the entertainment industry behind the scenes.

DATA
Alien: A humanoid female. About 170 cm (5 ft. 7 in.) tall. Blond hair and facial features of a fashion model.

Location of the luminous object at 20 seconds and every 5 seconds thereafter. It turned around as it moved downward.

| 2019.5.2 Thu. |

(The Space Soul of) Michael

Video | The reading was conducted on the spot

RYUHO OKAWA: I think I sense a small UFO. Who are you? [*About five seconds of silence*.] Your name is **"Michael"**?

MICHAEL: **We have been asked to help Happy Science and the Happiness Realization Party establish justice on Earth because they have been active with a very keen interest in the Asian and international affairs from the view of Japanese politics.**

INTERVIEWER A: Do you have a connection to Archangel Michael whose name is known widely on Earth?

MICHAEL: **We are spiritually connected to each other. Michael, also, has a space soul.**

  Lucifer is now drawing spiritual energy from Ahriman and Kandahar in space. So, I must develop a relationship with other space beings to fight them.

DATA
Alien: Blond hair and a fair face. Wears a tailcoat like a French military officer. About 2 m (6 ft. 6 in.) tall.
UFO: It is close to diamond-shaped with a hemispherical dome on top. It can board 15. In the sky above is a mother ship about 500 m (1640 ft.) long that came from the dark side of the Moon.

| 2019.5.2 Thu. |

Planet Elder in the Magellanic Galaxy: Yaidron 13

Video | The reading was conducted on the spot

YAIDRON: **This is Yaidron. It's been a while, but I'm back to protecting you again.**

INTERVIEWER A: Thank you. Did you know Michael was here a short while ago?

YAIDRON: **Yes, yes. I was listening to him. Michael came, and Yaidron came. In one meaning, we are trying to beef up our defense against Lucifer.**

A: Ahriman was here the other day.

YAIDRON: **Yes. We believe you will likely face tougher enemies than Lucifer.**

A: Is Michael's sense of justice similar to yours?

YAIDRON: **Actually, he is more political. We trust our intuition and take action, rather than acting politically.**

A: Then, are you closer to Metatron?

YAIDRON: **He is a little stronger in the aspect of love. As for us, we are cool. Cool and sometimes fiery.**

A: How do you see Japan's current sense of justice?

YAIDRON: **Umm. They have a weak sense of justice. Very weak. They are limp like sea cucumbers. So, they often cannot make judgment unless we help.**

A: Is that one of the reasons El Cantare is now working here in Japan?

YAIDRON: **Yes. But I am now a servant of El Cantare. I am doing my job as a servant.**

A: But Japanese people also have good points, right? "Harmony" is one thing they can boast to the world.

YAIDRON: **Yes. Of course, they do. But there are times when they must fight.**
   Anyway, we are working hard.

A: We really appreciate it.

DATA
UFO: It is shaped like an octopus dumpling (or a ping pong ball) with a straw hat on top. It can board 35.

The location and color of the luminous object at 30 seconds and every 10 seconds thereafter.

The flight path of Yaidron's UFO as it changed its color

The location and color of the luminous object at 361 seconds and every 5 seconds thereafter. It emitted different colors of light and turned around as it moved downward.

Index of Space People

It includes their nicknames.

A:
Aman 22
Amemiko 107
Angulimala (Tortootsie) 106

B:
Bazooka 56, 70, 71, 72, 81

E:
Eternal Beauty 55

F:
Friedrich 23

G:
Goeppels .... (36), 53, 94

H:
Hunter Queen 45

I:
Iktron 94
Indra 47

K:
Karl Jaspers 34
Knightmayor 43

L:
Liu Bei 19, 24, 28, 32, 90

M:
Maitrey 46, 48
Maitreya 108
Marvel 18
Master R (R. A. Goal) 40, 41
McCartney 50, 52, 76, 78, 92
Metatron 86, 89, 97, 102, 111
Michael (the space soul) 110, 111
Mille-feuille 92
Millennium II 44
Mr. R (R. A. Goal) 40, 41
Mycenae 72

N:
Namiel 31
New Yorker 79
Nichaetatron 104

R:
R. A. Goal 40, 41

S:
Saitron 103
Sandra 32
Santos 99
Semrozay 103

T:
Tortootsie (Angulimala) 106

W:
White 75

Y:
Yaidron 30, 31, 42, 46, 48, 49, 56, 60, 62, 64, 66, 69, 71, 72, 79, 80, 95, 100, 111
Yamrozay (Yamoozay) 86, 102

Index of Stars, Constellations, and Other Celestial Bodies

A:
Andalucia Beta in Ursa Minor 40, 41
Andromeda Galaxy 74, 82

B:
Bergius 99
Beta in the Magellanic Galaxy 56, 70

D:
Denken 23

E:
Elder in the Magellanic Galaxy 30, 31, 42, 46, 48, 49, 56, 60, 62, 64, 66, 69, 71, 72, 80, 95, 100, 111
Energy in the Andromeda Galaxy 47
Engel in Pisces 36, 53, 94

F:
From the Mother Ship near Venus 78

H:
Honeykaney in Scorpius 72

I:
Include in Sagittarius 86, 102, 103
Indole in Delphinus 43
Inuyasha in Cassiopeia 91

J:
Jupiter 54

K:
Kirolyn in Leo 105

M:
Mars 45
Michaeta in Pisces 94
Migel in Delphinus 50, 52, 76, 78, 93
Mint (near Altair) 54
Mohican in Capricornus 79
Moon 55

N:
Needle in Cancer 82
Next in Cassiopeia 44
Nibiru 18, 32
Nix in the Small Magellanic Cloud 19, 24, 28, 32, 90

O:
Orihime in Lyra 55
Orion 107

P:
Pixel in Andromeda Galaxy 106

S:
Sachertorte 92
Santhor 77
Serpent in Cygnus 54
Southern 75, 92
Spicy in Canis Major 20
Sympathy in Draco Albus 34

T:
The Fourth Planet in the Pleiades 105
The Pleiades 108
The Seventh Planet Mew in Lyra 105
The Third Star (γ) in Bergius 104, 105
Titan, One of the Satellites of Saturn ... 22

U:
UFOs Guiding Europe 30

V:
Vega 21

W:
Workthrough 51

ABOUT THE AUTHOR

RYUHO OKAWA was born on July 7th 1956, in Tokushima, Japan. After graduating from the University of Tokyo with a law degree, he joined a Tokyo-based trading house. While working at its New York headquarters, he studied international finance at the Graduate Center of the City University of New York. In 1981, he attained Great Enlightenment and became aware that he is El Cantare with a mission to bring salvation to all humankind. In 1986, he established Happy Science. It now has members in over 160 countries across the world, with more than 700 local branches and temples as well as 10,000 missionary houses around the world. The total number of lectures has exceeded 3,350 (of which more than 150 are in English) and over 2,850 books (of which more than 600 are Spiritual Interview Series) have been published, many of which are translated into 37 languages. Many of the books, including *The Laws of the Sun* have become best sellers or million sellers. To date, Happy Science has produced 23 movies. The original story and original concept were given by the Executive Producer Ryuho Okawa. Recent movie titles are *Beautiful Lure–A Modern Tale of "Painted Skin"* (live-action, May 2021), *Into the Dreams... and Horror Experiences* (live-action, August 2021), and *The Laws of the Universe–The Age of Elohim* (animation movie, October 2021). He has also composed the lyrics and music of over 450 songs, such as theme songs and featured songs of movies. Moreover, he is the Founder of Happy Science University and Happy Science Academy (Junior and Senior High School), Founder and President of the Happiness Realization Party, Founder and Honorary Headmaster of Happy Science Institute of Government and Management, Founder of IRH Press Co., Ltd., and the Chairperson of NEW STAR PRODUCTION Co., Ltd. and ARI Production Co., Ltd.

Who is El Cantare?

EL CANTARE

ALPHA

330 MILLION YEARS AGO

A part of the core consciousness of El Cantare who descended to Earth around 330 million years ago. Alpha preached Earth's Truths to harmonize and unify Earth-born humans and space people who came from other planets.

ELOHIM

150 MILLION YEARS AGO

A part of El Cantare's core consciousness who descended to Earth around 150 million years ago. He gave wisdom, mainly on the differences of light and darkness, good and evil.

RYUHO OKAWA

EL CANTARE means "the Light of the Earth," and is the Supreme God of the Earth who has been guiding humankind since the beginning of Genesis. He is whom Jesus called Father and Muhammad called Allah, and is the Creator in Shintoism, *Ame-no-Mioya-Gami*. Different parts of El Cantare's core consciousness have descended to Earth in the past, once as Alpha and another as Elohim. His branch spirits, such as Shakyamuni Buddha and Hermes, have descended to Earth many times and helped to flourish many civilizations. To unite various religions and to integrate various fields of study in order to build a new civilization on Earth, a part of the core consciousness has descended to Earth as Master Ryuho Okawa.

HIS SOUL SIBLINGS

RA MU was a leader who built the golden age of the civilization of Mu around 17,000 years ago. As a religious leader and a politician, he ruled by uniting religion and politics.

Ra Mu
17,000 years ago

Thoth
12,000 years ago

Rient Arl Croud
7,000 years ago

Ophealis
6,500 years ago

Hermes
4,300 years ago

Gautama Siddhartha
2,600 years ago

THOTH was an almighty leader who built the golden age of the Atlantic civilization around 12,000 years ago. In the Egyptian mythology, he is known as god Thoth.

RIENT ARL CROUD was born as a king of the ancient Incan Empire around 7,000 years ago and taught about the mysteries of the mind. In the heavenly world, he is responsible for the interactions that take place between various planets.

OPHEALIS was born in Greece around 6,500 years ago and was the leader who took an expedition to as far as Egypt. He is the God of miracles, prosperity, and arts, and is known as Osiris in the Egyptian mythology.

HERMES is one of the 12 Olympian gods in Greek mythology, but the spiritual Truth is that he taught the teachings of love and progress around 4,300 years ago that became the origin of the current Western civilization. He is a hero that truly existed.

GAUTAMA SIDDHARTHA (SHAKYAMUNI BUDDHA) was born as a prince into the Shakya Clan in India around 2,600 years ago. When he was 29 years old, he renounced the world and sought enlightenment. He later attained Great Enlightenment and founded Buddhism.

ABOUT HAPPY SCIENCE

Happy Science is a global movement that empowers individuals to find purpose and spiritual happiness and to share that happiness with their families, societies, and the world. With more than 12 million members around the world, Happy Science aims to increase awareness of spiritual truths and expand our capacity for love, compassion, and joy so that together we can create the kind of world we all wish to live in.

Activities at Happy Science are based on the Principles of Happiness (Love, Wisdom, Self-Reflection, and Progress). These principles embrace worldwide philosophies and beliefs, transcending boundaries of culture and religions.

Love teaches us to give ourselves freely without expecting anything in return; it encompasses giving, nurturing, and forgiving.

Wisdom leads us to the insights of spiritual truths, and opens us to the true meaning of life and the will of God (the universe, the highest power, Buddha).

Self-Reflection brings a mindful, nonjudgmental lens to our thoughts and actions to help us find our truest selves—the essence of our souls—and deepen our connection to the highest power. It helps us attain a clean and peaceful mind and leads us to the right life path.

Progress emphasizes the positive, dynamic aspects of our spiritual growth—actions we can take to manifest and spread happiness around the world. It's a path that not only expands our soul growth, but also furthers the collective potential of the world we live in.

PROGRAMS AND EVENTS

The doors of Happy Science are open to all. We offer a variety of programs and events, including self-exploration and self-growth programs, spiritual seminars, meditation and contemplation sessions, study groups, and book events.

Our programs are designed to:
* Deepen your understanding of your purpose and meaning in life
* Improve your relationships and increase your capacity to love unconditionally
* Attain peace of mind, decrease anxiety and stress, and feel positive
* Gain deeper insights and a broader perspective on the world
* Learn how to overcome life's challenges
  ... and much more.

For more information, visit happy-science.org.

CONTACT INFORMATION

Happy Science is a worldwide organization with faith centers around the globe. For a comprehensive list of centers, visit the worldwide directory at *happy-science.org*. The following are some of the many Happy Science locations:

UNITED STATES AND CANADA

New York
79 Franklin St., New York, NY 10013
Phone: 212-343-7972
Fax: 212-343-7973
Email: ny@happy-science.org
Website: happyscience-usa.org

New Jersey
725 River Rd, #102B, Edgewater, NJ 07020
Phone: 201-313-0127
Fax: 201-313-0120
Email: nj@happy-science.org
Website: happyscience-usa.org

Florida
5208 8th St., Zephyrhills, FL 33542
Phone: 813-715-0000
Fax: 813-715-0010
Email: florida@happy-science.org
Website: happyscience-usa.org

Atlanta
1874 Piedmont Ave., NE Suite 360-C
Atlanta, GA 30324
Phone: 404-892-7770
Email: atlanta@happy-science.org
Website: happyscience-usa.org

San Francisco
525 Clinton St.
Redwood City, CA 94062
Phone & Fax: 650-363-2777
Email: sf@happy-science.org
Website: happyscience-usa.org

Los Angeles
1590 E. Del Mar Blvd., Pasadena, CA 91106
Phone: 626-395-7775
Fax: 626-395-7776
Email: la@happy-science.org
Website: happyscience-usa.org

Orange County
10231 Slater Ave., #204
Fountain Valley, CA 92708
Phone: 714-659-1501
Email: oc@happy-science.org
Website: happyscience-usa.org

San Diego
7841 Balboa Ave., Suite #202
San Diego, CA 92111
Phone: 626-395-7775
Fax: 626-395-7776
E-mail: sandiego@happy-science.org
Website: happyscience-usa.org

Hawaii
Phone: 808-591-9772
Fax: 808-591-9776
Email: hi@happy-science.org
Website: happyscience-usa.org

Kauai
3343 Kanakolu Street, Suite 5
Lihue, HI 96766, U.S.A.
Phone: 808-822-7007
Fax: 808-822-6007
Email: kauai-hi@happy-science.org
Website: happyscience-usa.org

Toronto
845 The Queensway
Etobicoke ON M8Z 1N6 Canada
Phone: 1-416-901-3747
Email: toronto@happy-science.org
Website: happy-science.ca

Vancouver
#201-2607 East 49th Avenue
Vancouver, BC, V5S 1J9, Canada
Phone: 1-604-437-7735
Fax: 1-604-437-7764
Email: vancouver@happy-science.org
Website: happy-science.ca

INTERNATIONAL

Tokyo
1-6-7 Togoshi, Shinagawa
Tokyo, 142-0041 Japan
Phone: 81-3-6384-5770
Fax: 81-3-6384-5776
Email: tokyo@happy-science.org
Website: happy-science.org

Seoul
74, Sadang-ro 27-gil,
Dongjak-gu, Seoul, Korea
Phone: 82-2-3478-8777
Fax: 82-2-3478-9777
Email: korea@happy-science.org
Website: happyscience-korea.org

London
3 Margaret St.
London, W1W 8RE United Kingdom
Phone: 44-20-7323-9255
Fax: 44-20-7323-9344
Email: eu@happy-science.org
Website: happyscience-uk.org

Taipei
No. 89, Lane 155, Dunhua N. Road
Songshan District, Taipei City 105, Taiwan
Phone: 886-2-2719-9377
Fax: 886-2-2719-5570
Email: taiwan@happy-science.org
Website: happyscience-tw.org

Sydney
516 Pacific Hwy, Lane Cove North,
NSW 2066, Australia
Phone: 61-2-9411-2877
Fax: 61-2-9411-2822
Email: sydney@happy-science.org

Malaysia
No 22A, Block 2, Jalil Link Jalan Jalil
Jaya 2, Bukit Jalil 57000, Kuala Lumpur, Malaysia
Phone: 60-3-8998-7877
Fax: 60-3-8998-7977
Email: malaysia@happy-science.org
Website: happyscience.org.my

Brazil Headquarters
Rua. Domingos de Morais 1154,
Vila Mariana, Sao Paulo SP
CEP 04010-100, Brazil
Phone: 55-11-5088-3800
Email: sp@happy-science.org
Website: happyscience.com.br

Nepal
Kathmandu Metropolitan City Ward
No. 15,
Ring Road, Kimdol,
Sitapaila Kathmandu, Nepal
Phone: 97-714-272931
Email: nepal@happy-science.org

Jundiai
Rua Congo, 447, Jd. Bonfiglioli
Jundiai-CEP, 13207-340
Phone: 55-11-4587-5952
Email: jundiai@happy-science.org

Uganda
Plot 877 Rubaga Road, Kampala
P.O. Box 34130, Kampala, Uganda
Phone: 256-79-4682-121
Email: uganda@happy-science.org
Website: happyscience-uganda.org

ABOUT IRH PRESS

IRH Press Co., Ltd., based in Tokyo, was founded in 1987 as a publishing division of Happy Science. IRH Press publishes religious and spiritual books, journals, magazines and also operates broadcast and film production enterprises. For more information, visit *okawabooks.com*.

Follow us on:

Facebook: Okawa Books   Twitter: Okawa Books
Goodreads: Ryuho Okawa   Instagram: OkawaBooks
Pinterest: Okawa Books

NEWSLETTER

To receive book related news, promotions and events, please subscribe to our newsletter below.

 https://okawabooks.us11.list-manage.com/subscribe?u=1fc70960eefd92668052ab7f8&id=2fbd8150ef

MEDIA

OKAWA BOOK CLUB

 A conversation about Ryuho Okawa's titles, topics ranging from self-help, current affairs, spirituality and religions.

Available at iTunes, Spotify and Amazon Music.

Apple iTunes:
https://podcasts.apple.com/us/podcast/okawa-book-club/id1527893043

Spotify:
https://open.spotify.com/show/09mpgX2iJ6stVm4eBRdo2b

Amazon Music:
https://music.amazon.com/podcasts/7b759f24-ff72-4523-bfee-24f48294998f/Okawa-Book-Club

BOOKS BY RYUHO OKAWA

RYUHO OKAWA'S LAWS SERIES

The Laws Series is an annual volume of books that are mainly comprised of Ryuho Okawa's lectures on various topics that highlight principles and guidelines for the activities of Happy Science every year. *The Laws of the Sun*, the first publication of the laws series, ranked in the annual best-selling list in Japan in 1987. Since then, all of the laws series' titles have ranked in the annual best-selling list for more than two decades, setting socio-cultural trends in Japan and around the world.

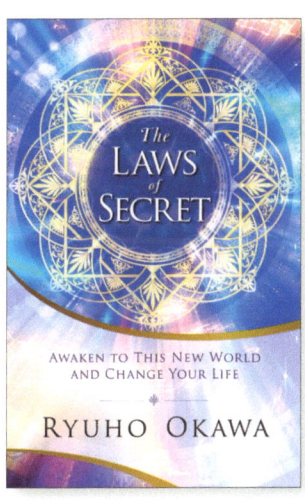

The 27th Laws Series
THE LAWS OF SECRET

AWAKEN TO THIS NEW WORLD AND CHANGE YOUR LIFE

Paperback • 248 pages • $16.95
ISBN: 978-1-942125-81-5

Our physical world coexists with the multi-dimensional spirit world and we are constantly interacting with some kind of spiritual energy, whether positive or negative, without consciously realizing it. This book reveals how our lives are affected by invisible influences, including the spiritual reasons behind influenza, the novel coronavirus infection, and other illnesses.

The new view of the world in this book will inspire you to change your life in a better direction, and to become someone who can give hope and courage to others in this age of confusion.

LAWS SERIES

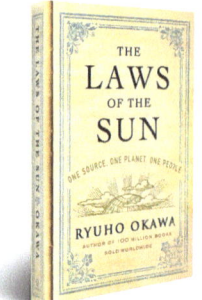

THE LAWS OF THE SUN
ONE SOURCE, ONE PLANET, ONE PEOPLE

Paperback • 288 pages • $15.95 ISBN: 978-1-942125-43-3

Imagine if you could ask God why he created this world and what spiritual laws he used to shape us—and everything around us. In *The Laws of the Sun*, Okawa outlines these laws of the universe and provides a road map for living one's life with greater purpose and meaning. This powerful book shows the way to realize true happiness—a happiness that continues from this world through the other.

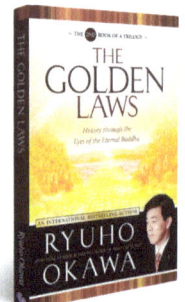

THE GOLDEN LAWS
HISTORY THROUGH THE EYES OF THE ETERNAL BUDDHA

Paperback • 201 pages • $14.95 ISBN: 978-1-941779-81-1

Throughout history, Great Guiding Spirits of Light have been present on Earth in both the East and the West at crucial points in human history to further our spiritual development. *The Golden Laws* reveals how Divine Plan has been unfolding on Earth, and outlines 5,000 years of the secret history of humankind. Once we understand the true course of history, through past, present and into the future, we cannot help but become aware of the significance of our spiritual mission in the present age.

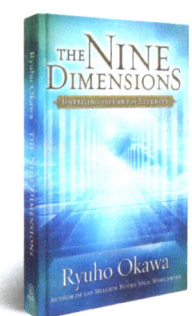

THE NINE DIMENSIONS
UNVEILING THE LAWS OF ETERNITY

Paperback • 168 pages • $15.95   ISBN: 978-0-982698-56-3

This book is a window into the mind of our loving God, who designed this world and the vast, wondrous world of our afterlife as a school with many levels through which our souls learn and grow. When the religions and cultures of the world discover the truth of their common spiritual origin, they will be inspired to accept their differences, come together under faith in God, and build an era of harmony and peaceful progress on Earth.

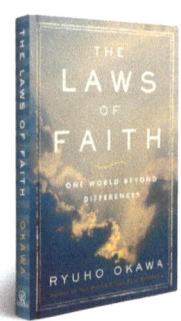

THE LAWS OF FAITH
ONE WORLD BEYOND DIFFERENCES

Paperback • 208 pages • $15.95   ISBN: 978-1-942125-34-1

Ryuho Okawa preaches at the core of a new universal religion from various angles while integrating logical and spiritual viewpoints in mind with current world situations. This book offers us the key to accept diversities beyond differences in ethnicity, religion, race, gender, descent, and so on, harmonize the individuals and nations and create a world filled with peace and prosperity.

RECOMMENDED SPIRITUAL MESSAGES

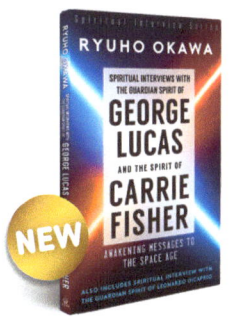

Spiritual Interviews with the Guardian Spirit of George Lucas and the Spirit of Carrie Fisher
Awakening Messages to the Space Age

Paperback • 154 pages • $11.95 ISBN: 978-1943928149

In the world today, a large totalitarian nation is aiming to take control of the world, while small democratic powers are trying to resist its attack. By reading this book, you will realize that similar battles were already happening in outer space, and that the *Star Wars Series* is a saga based on the real-life stories.

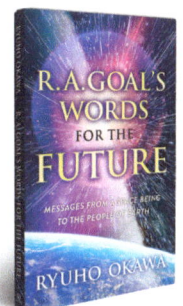

R. A. GOAL'S WORDS FOR THE FUTURE
MESSAGES FROM A SPACE BEING TO THE PEOPLE OF EARTH

Paperback • 174 pages • $11.95   ISBN: 978-1-943928-10-1

R. A. Goal, a certified messiah from Planet Andalucia Beta in Ursa Minor, gives humans on Earth three predictions for 2021. They include the prospect of the novel coronavirus pandemic, the outlook of economic crisis, and the risk of war. But the hope is that Savior is now born on Earth to overcome any bad predictions. Now is the time to open our hearts and listen to the words from R. A. Goal.

WITH SAVIOR
MESSAGES FROM SPACE BEING YAIDRON

Paperback • 232 pages • $13.95   ISBN: 978-1-943869-94-7

The human race is now faced with multiple unprecedented crises. Perhaps God is warning us humans to reconsider our materialistic and arrogant ways. Fortunately, God has sent us a savior, who is now teaching us to repent and showing us the path we should choose. In this book, space being Yaidron sends his warnings and messages of hope.

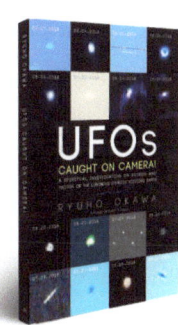

UFOs Caught on Camera!
A Spiritual Investigation of the Luminous Objects Visiting Earth

Paperback • 112 pages • $17.95 ISBN: 978-1943869312

In the Summer of 2018, over 60 types of UFOs appeared before the author. UFOs Caught on Camera! is a detailed compilation of Okawa's sightings, with visual analysis of the luminous objects visiting Earth and spiritually sourced commentary of the extraterrestrial intelligence behind them.

For a complete list of books, visit okawabooks.com

THE ESSENCE OF BUDDHA
The Path to Enlightenment

THE LAWS OF HOPE
The Light is Here

SPIRITUAL WORLD 101
A guide to a spiritually happy life

ALIEN INVASION
Can We Defend Earth?

THE SHAPE OF THINGS IN 2100
H.G. Wells Predicts the Future of the World

INVINCIBLE THINKING
An Essential Guide for a Lifetime of
Growth, Success, and Triumph

THINK BIG!
Be Positive and Be Brave to Achieve Your Dreams

CHANGE YOUR LIFE, CHANGE THE WORLD
A Spiritual Guide to Living Now

SECRETS OF THE EVERLASTING TRUTHS
A New Paradigm for Living on Earth

MUSIC BY RYUHO OKAWA

THE THUNDER -a composition for repelling the Coronavirus-

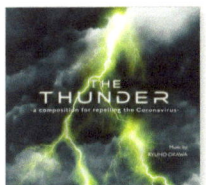

We have been granted this music from our Lord. It will repel away the novel Coronavirus originated in China. Experience this magnificent powerful music.

Search on YouTube
the thunder coronavirus for a short ad!

THE EXORCISM -prayer music for repelling Lost Spirits-

Feel the divine vibrations of this Japanese and Western exorcising symphony to banish all evil possessions you suffer from and to purify your space!

Search on YouTube
the exorcism repelling for a short ad!

WITH SAVIOR (English version)
"Come what may, you shall expect your future"

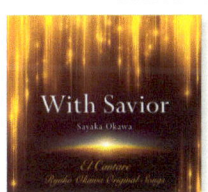

This is the message of hope to the modern people who are living in the midst of the Coronavirus pandemic, natural disasters, economic depression, and other various crises.

Search on YouTube
with savior for a short ad!

THE WATER REVOLUTION (English and Chinese version)
"Power to the People!"

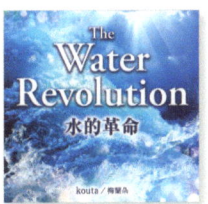

For the truth and happiness of the 1.4 billion people in China who have no freedom. Love, justice, and sacred rage of God are on this melody that will give you courage to fight to bring peace.

Search on YouTube
the water revolution for a short ad!

☞LISTEN NOW TODAY!

◎Download from Spotify iTunes Amazon ...and more!

CD available at amazon.com, and Happy Science local branches & shoja (temples)

www.ingramcontent.com/pod-product-compliance
Lightning Source LLC
Chambersburg PA
CBHW040515130526
44592CB00045B/5